Detente Diplomacy: United States and European Security in the 1970's

Timothy W. Stanley
Darnell M. Whitt

Published for the
Atlantic Council
of the United States

Foreword by
Livingston T. Merchant

Detente Diplomacy: United States and European Security in the 1970's

D849
57

The Dunellen Company, Inc., New York

International Standard Book Number 0-8424-0003-6.

Library of Congress catalog card number 72-119339.

Printed in the United States of America.

Designed by Anspak Grossman Portugal, Inc.

For Terry and Christopher
and
for M. P. W.

Contents

About the Authors

Foreword

Detente Diplomacy: United States and European Security in the 1970's is the result of our concern at the Atlantic Council of the United States to provide a brief, objective, and timely analysis of American options with regard to European security in the context of changing East-West relations during the next decade. The book was prepared by Timothy W. Stanley and Darnell M. Whitt, in consultation with an advisory committee of the Atlantic Council that included Theodore C. Achilles, Charles E. Bohlen, W. Randolph Burgess, Robert L. Dennison, William C. Foster, Alfred M. Gruenther, Joseph W. Harned, Livingston Hartley, John D. Hickerson, Robert S. Jordan, Foy D. Kohler, Lyman L. Lemnitzer, Garrison Norton, Eugene V. Rostow, Cortlandt V. R. Schuyler, Marshall D. Shulman, Llewellyn E. Thompson, William R. Tyler, Richard J. Wallace, Thomas W. Wilson, Jr., and myself. Because of the current state of flux and the many new developments in the central issues of European and Atlantic security, it should be noted that the book went to press on March 1, 1970.

The Atlantic Council wishes to thank members of the advisory committee for their valuable comments and suggestions during the meetings. Several comments by members of the group are included in an appendix to the monograph *A Conference on European Security?—Problems, Prospects, and Pitfalls*, by Dr. Stanley, published earlier this spring by the Council. The substantive views expressed in this book are, of course, the responsibility of the authors. The Atlantic Council is responsible for its presentation to the public.

As a former official involved in American foreign policy and Western diplomacy, I am aware how easily the complex issues can become oversimplified in the press and in the public mind. I am therefore pleased that the authors of this book have been able to present the current issues and proposals for action not only in historical perspective and analytical detail but also in the context of contemporary international politics.

It is the Council's hope that Dr. Stanley and Mr. Whitt's book will prove to be a useful contribution to the study of a subject that is important as well as complex, and of great current interest.

Livingston T. Merchant
Chairman
Atlantic Council of
the United States

Washington, D. C.
March 1, 1970

Acknowledgments

We are very much indebted to the Atlantic Council of the United States for their sponsorship of this project, which also included a shorter treatment of the security conference aspects in a monograph published earlier this spring. Both publications benefited greatly from the encouragement and comments of the Council's advisory group, chaired by Ambassador Merchant. Messrs. Achilles, Burgess, and Wallace rendered invaluable help throughout; and the primary credit for the speedy, and therefore timely, publication goes to Joseph W. Harned, Assistant Director of the Council (with that credit, however, must go a share of blame for any errors ascribable to Joe Harned's flogging the tired authors with deadlines—as well as our thanks for his own unflagging energies and ability), and of course to the publishers, in the persons of Eugene H. Nellen and Paule H. Jones. The production side was greatly aided by the skill of several typists, but we owe special thanks to Elaine Clark of the Washington Center for Foreign Policy Research and June Haley of the Atlantic Council, both of whom labored cheerfully into the small hours of several mornings.

Several of our colleagues at the Washington Center gave us the benefit of their advice, both individually and collectively; and their insights were most helpful. We also gratefully acknowledge the contributions of former Ambassador Harlan Cleveland, who made available to us the manuscript of his forthcoming book *The Transatlantic Bargain* and who, during our association at NATO, stimulated a number of the ideas presented in this book.

The Institute for Strategic Studies kindly granted permission to reprint "The Military Balance between NATO and the Warsaw Pact" from the 1969-1970 edition of *The Military Balance*, which can be obtained from the Institute, 18 Adam Street, London, WC2. Their cooperation is especially appreciated.

Finally, we both wish to make clear that there is no connection between the views expressed in this book, which are our responsibility alone, and any official views of the U.S. Government or NATO. While our government background, obviously has added to our understanding of the problems covered, the book is entirely an independent endeavor, researched from public sources. Because of the vast amount of literature on the subject, we have included some bibliographic comments in the notes, in the expectation that they—and the documentary material in the Appendixes—will be helpful to specialists and researchers. And we hope the general reader of the text will find it a useful guide to a vital if complex subject, which promises to be moving rapidly across the headlines during the 1970's.

Detente Diplomacy: United States and European Security in the 1970's

Europe

1 Introduction: The Current Scene

The spring of 1970 is already an active one in European security matters: resolutions in the Senate for a "substantial withdrawal" of American forces from Europe are a focus of public concern; the United States and the Soviet Union resume their crucial talks on strategic arms limitation at Vienna on April 16; in late May the NATO Foreign Ministers hold their spring meeting in Rome—where they seem likely to focus on the "detente" aspects of East-West relations.

West Germany's *Ostpolitik*, led by Chancellor Brandt, has involved exploratory negotiations on critical subjects with East Germany, Poland, and Czechoslovakia, as well as Russia. Meanwhile, the United States, Britain, France, and the Soviet Union are exchanging invitations to discuss the Berlin problem; West Germany's steel-pipe-for-natural-gas deal is the largest ever between a Communist and a Western country, even larger than that of Italy's Fiat; and the Soviet and American governments have just concluded a major renewal of their cultural exchange agreement. In the wings, the Warsaw Pact's proposal for a European security conference waits its cue for another entry on stage, while NATO may be preparing to offer serious negotiations on mutual and balanced force reductions.

At the same time, despite these appearances of diplomatic movement, the central issues of European security, which have divided East and West for over two decades, remain unsolved and show little in the way of basic change.

The Soviet compaign for a new East-West security conference grows out of the long struggle for political influence and international stability in Europe. This campaign reached its high watermark at the end of 1969, following a

1

steady buildup starting with the Budapest appeal of March and culminating
with the Prague statement in October—immediately after the West German
elections had given birth to the new coalition's *Ostpolitik*. The West's
reaction to the campaign has been cool: NATO ignored the Budapest
invitation in its twentieth anniversary communique in April 1969—being
aided in so doing by an extraordinary statement by TASS, the Soviet press
agency, timed to hit the Ministerial meeting just as the conference idea was to
be discussed by the Western powers. This cold war blast, preceded by major
Russian naval maneuvers in the Atlantic, soon froze the slightly warmer air
which had moved in from Budapest, causing more than one observer to
wonder whether that endeavor had not been primarily designed as a
distraction from the 1968 invasion of Czechoslovakia.

In December 1969, NATO Foreign Ministers faced the specific two-point
agenda for an East-West conference proposed by the Pact at Prague: mutual
renunciations of force; and "expansion of trade, economic, scientific and
technical relations on the principle of equal rights" (meaning legal recognition
of the East German regime). American Secretary of State Rogers called this
agenda "nebulous and imprecise" and opposed an "unrealistic and premature" exercise. The NATO Ministers took a cautious view as well; but their
formal declaration on the subject left the door open to a search for genuine
progress on European security through multilateral as well as bilateral
negotiations.

The 1970 season opened with an unusual Russian press conference, which
for the first time officially dropped the theme of an all-European conference
as one in which Russia would take part but foreign states like the United
States and Canada would not. Moreover, the urgency of holding a major
East-West conference in the first half of 1970—indeed, the government of
Finland had formally offered to sponsor such an assembly early this
year—faded into the latter part of 1970 or early 1971. Simultaneously,
dispatches from Eastern capitals began to show new internal splits developing
in the views of the East Europeans and reflected earlier references to a
peoples' congress, an event traditionally associated more with agitprop and
Communist Party activities than with interstate diplomacy.

A review of Soviet foreign policy since World War II shows that the
"conference" note has been played in a variety of different chord
combinations, from atonal anti-German revanchism or anti-Americanism to a
harmonious pan-European peace and disarmament motif. It has simultaneously been directed outwardly at the West, as a siren call of detente, and
inwardly at the Communist world's own counterpoint. Its apparent dormancy
as the new year opened is probably misleading for just this reason. Given the
problems and limited options open to Moscow, the security conference

concept is a useful variety of carrot which alternates with the stick in the East's "Westpolitik," and perhaps it also has a preemptive role vis-à-vis the *Ostpolitik* of Chancellor Brandt. In the East it is supported, albeit for widely different reasons, by Ulbricht's East Germany (if he can thereby gain international status) and Ceausescu's Rumania (to attain maneuver room from Moscow). It may thus represent, in effect, a lowest common denominator of Warsaw Pact agreement. One can therefore confidently expect that the conference proposal will be revived, repainted and relaunched in whatever direction seems most useful to its proponents—in the not too distant future.

The United States enters the current period of "detente diplomacy" about European security in a new mood. It is well characterized in President Nixon's State of the World message as calling for a lower American profile in the world. But while the loss of any delusions of America's omniscience—even of omnipotence—is good news for many, the world's issues and problems remain. And they are not likely to disappear; although they will be altered, perhaps for the worse, by the doubling of world population expected by the end of the century.

The Nixon pronouncements have been criticized more for their level of generality and the lack of hard policy judgments than for their nonheroic and nonmessianic flavor. But the policy choices that eventually must be made will inevitably reflect the reactions of others to the new profile. Will Russia match the willingness to negotiate? Will our allies accept the obligations of partnership? And will Congress finance the President's efforts to maintain strength? And if not, what are the consequences? For as the President said, our security is inseparable from Europe's and "we can no more disengage from Europe than from Alaska."

A valid and viable security settlement in Europe, however difficult to achieve, might prove to be a critical watershed: beyond it could lie either a mere substitution of other arenas of conflict or, perhaps, a radical change for the better in Soviet attitudes toward world politics and problems. Such a dominance of ideology by pragmatism would constitute a revolution of sorts in Soviet Communism. But, it is said, we live in a revolutionary age. And it is just possible that the Western "revolutions" in perceptions will prove contagious. One must therefore keep an eye on the long term, in this sense, while in the meantime getting on with a realistic approach to East-West issues.

If one were to depict the theme of this book in a drawing, it would show two duelers, astride a map of Europe, one facing East and one West, each clad half in diplomatic stripes, half in military uniform. The Western gladiator might be parrying an outthrust Picasso peace dove with his NATO shield, while thrusting with an olive branch in his other hand. This, in turn would be neatly parried with the hammer and sickle flag. But to be accurate, the picture would also have to show a sword in each belt, and a pistol in each holster. And the obvious caption would have to be "En garde!" That "duel" is what this book is all about.

2 The Actors on the European Security Stage

For centuries Europe has been not only the cradle of Western civilization but also the incubator of its conflicts—feudal, religious, dynastic, imperial, or nationalistic. Europe's last great civil war, as World War II has been called, brought a major change of uncertain duration: Europe became the object rather than the subject of power after the defeat of the Axis and in light of the exhaustion of the European Allies. The resulting vacuum proved irresistible to Russian power; national goals, such as the desire for a more secure western frontier and access to the sea, and the international ideology of Communism—both reinforced each other vis-à-vis Western Europe.

It is rather ironic that twenty-five years after the war a revisionist literature[1] depicts Stalin as a reluctant participant, if not indeed a victim of a Western-instigated cold war.* Roosevelt's prediction to Stalin that he could not keep American forces in Europe for more than a year or two after the war was borne out; the combined strength of the United States, Britain, and Canada dropped from nearly five million men under arms in Europe in 1945 to under nine hundred thousand in 1946.

Russia, by contrast, reduced its force of four million very little—leaving a rather impressive four-to-one ratio with which to consolidate control of Eastern Europe and project Soviet influence into Western Europe, despite America's fledgling atomic power. Between 1940 and 1946, the Soviet Union managed to annex parts of five countries and all of the three Baltic republics, totalling nearly two million square miles and twenty-four million people.

---

*America's strong anti-Communist mood of the late 1940's and early 1950's may have overexaggerated the threat and thereby led to a Russian overreaction, but the historical record is quite clear about the early postwar period. To conclude, as some revisionists apparently do, that the East was merely blustering out of a concern for its own security requires one to overlook Soviet actions and capabilities and to assume that ideological motivations and stated intentions were without influence on Soviet policies.

Having been drawn out of its interwar isolation and into Europe only by a direct armed attack (despite fairly clear evidence that American interests were threatened by the revisionist and expansionist ambitions of the Axis), the United States substantially withdrew again at war's end. The re-engagement process—the Truman Doctrine, the Marshall Plan, and NATO—came about as Soviet behavior in the United Nations and Russia's attitude toward the wartime understandings about Eastern Europe shattered Western hopes that great-power collaboration would survive the peace and that the United Nations could be an effective instrument of that collaboration for international peacekeeping.

The stakes then, as today, involved the political future of a continent which aggregates the world's third largest economic product (after the United States and the Soviet Union) and population (after China and India). The issues over Europe, as the sharpest focus of a global East-West dispute, have been muted by time and by a common perception that the employment of force between nuclear superpowers is dysfunctional at best and mutually disastrous at worst. None the less, the issues which evolved from World War II remain; they engage the vital interests of Europeans—Eastern and Western— Russians and Americans. The specifics of the substantive issues will be discussed in a later chapter, but it seems worth while to review the major actors on the scene and the role that each sees in relation to the stakes involved—a review of the names and numbers of the players, as a warm-up to the rules and the game itself.

The Soviet Union

The Soviet Union, like the United States, is Janus-faced, looking at Europe while simultaneously being an Asian power. Moscow, at the center of European Russia, sits exactly halfway between New York and Tokyo. All of the United States east of the Mississippi is closer to London and Paris than is fully one half of Russia. The Atlantic's three-thousand-mile width could be contained in Asian Russia alone. Thus, the Soviet claim to be a European power, in contrast to America, by virtue of geography alone has a somewhat lesser force in the jet age.

Historic Russia—that is, the land of the Great Russians—has been the eastern outpost of Western and Christian civilization since the early Middle Ages. From the time of Peter the Great and Catherine II, a bivalent love-hate, imitation-rejection pattern has characterized Russian attitudes toward the West; and this was only partially sublimated by the importation of Communism after World War I. Russia's drive to the sea had involved her in European politics—and conflicts, like the Crimean War—in the Eastern question, and in Far Eastern affairs, for example, the Russo-Japanese War.

Invaded by Napoleon, by the Germans in World War I, by the Western powers in 1918-1920, and finally by Hitler, Russia's historical perception of threat from the West identifies with Europe in general and Germany in particular. This is reinforced, of course, by ideological antipathy toward "capitalist-imperialist" states—especially toward the West Europeans, since they are linked with the United States, the world's only other military superpower and, by Soviet definition, the citadel of the political-economic system whose demise is a fundamental goal of Marxism-Leninism. Also it is the United States which now performs the containment role vis-à-vis Russia, which was a British preoccupation during the nineteenth century. Over and above a defensive and "preclusive" interest in Western Europe, there doubtless exists a hope of positive gain in the sense of access to resources, capital, and technology—if not by conquest, then by creating a favorable relation of forces, which in Soviet terminology determines the outcome of conflicting interests. As the following historical section shows, there has been a remarkable continuity of Soviet objectives and tactics in pursuing these goals in Western Europe.

But the defensive mentality, so often noted in Russian behavior, has another dimension as well. In Eastern Europe, the cordon sanitaire with which the Russians surrounded themselves after the war—in the form of Sovietized client-states consisting of some one hundred million people and four hundred thousand square miles—has manifested a recurrent nationalism despite two and one half decades of Communism. Poznan, Budapest, and Prague must symbolize to Moscow a dangerous long-term instability in its security system—a danger defined as any totalitarian state must define it: as schisms and heresies in orthodox ideological doctrine. And this fear is perhaps as good an explanation as any for the Soviet invasion of Czechoslovakia in August 1968.

From time to time, one encounters in the West the question of why the issues left unsettled more than two decades after World War II cannot now be put to rest; why, for example, the Russians, with their security of nuclear power and their admitted domestic needs and Far Eastern challenge, cannot bury the ideological rhetoric of the cold war about burying capitalism and seek more pragmatic, positive relations with the West.

Many experts would reply that the Soviets simply cannot do so, not so much out of dogmatic conviction—although Marxism-Leninism is proving to have a long "half-life" in the face of an accelerating irrelevance—as out of the ideological imperatives of the struggle for power within the Soviet system. Russians, it should be noted, are only about one half of the Soviet Union's population; it was not surprising that the "nationality question" was one of the first to be addressed by Lenin. From Moscow's point of view, it might seem that a break in the seamless security web could originate anywhere in Eastern Europe, unleash centrifugal forces, and lead to a breakup in the Soviet system itself, or at least to serious convulsions in its power structure.

Coincidentally, there are some signs, as this is being written, that a change in Soviet leadership may be shaping up, possibly in connection with the next Communist Party Congress.[2] But the system would remain the same, and the likely successors to Brezhnev and Kosygin are thought to be equally hard line, if not more so.

And then there is China, about which Russian insecurities go back seven centuries, to the Mongol hordes. The Sino-Soviet split permitted old national conflicts to resurface and, indeed, to be intensified by the ideological competition for leadership of international Communism. Although the Russian eastern-security question undoubtedly poses some incentives to seek stability on the Western front, that is in Europe, the issues there—especially the German question—may be too closely tied to historical fears, to ideology, and to Soviet insecurities and internal power struggles to permit real accommodation, at least in the immediate future.

The United States

America, as the child of Europe, also has a web of historic, cultural, and economic links with Western Europe which have twice brought American military intervention in defense of the balance of power in Europe. In one sense, NATO represented an effort to change the patterns of the past and meet the new threat from the East by engaging American power in European security on a semi-permanent basis. Thus, America became a European power—initially by her role in liberating it, and then again, following an initial demobilization and semidisengagement, by invitation in the late 1940's and early 1950's.

As the decade of the 1970's opens, America remains a European power by virtue of a vital interest in Europe's future, a large military presence on the continent, and two decades of working within an alliance whose very success has given rise to some of its current problems. Among European elites—at least those in the age group which recalls more than the postwar economic recovery and prosperity of Europe—there appears to be a striking persistence in the desire that America's role continue.[3]

Quite apart from patterns of tradition, belief, and European interest, the United States remains centrally concerned with European security—a fact sometimes lost on radicals of the younger generation who regard NATO as an anachronistic legacy from a history they do not understand and often regard as irrelevant to themselves.

European security is vital to the United States for a variety of reasons: First, there is the "preclusive" factor that Soviet dominance of Western Europe—whether by employment of military means or by European accommodation, as in the case of Finland—would create a "relation of forces"[4] which would favor the Soviet Union and would dangerously upset the global balance of power. Second, there is the positive need to engage Europe's technology, resources, and political traditions in solving the plethora of global problems which confront mankind in the remaining decades of this century. These problems range from the interaction of population, technology, and ecology, to development—and the "North-South" schism between the haves and the have-nots—and to the maintenance of relative stability in the international security system. America's post-Vietnam reassessment seems likely to devalue, for some years to come, the political viability of unilateral American action in a peacekeeping role. Even foreign aid proves increasingly burdensome to Congress. And President Nixon has undoubtedly captured the mood of the country with his low-profile approach.

In face of this apparent consensus on a nonheroic role for the United States in world affairs, it is hard to find other candidates for collective action who have the power to make more than token contributions and have the requisite will and inclination to act responsibly in the interests of the wider world community. The latter criterion would seem to exclude both China and the Soviet Union; Japan currently lacks the will and, in some areas, the necessary international acceptability; and India, Pakistan, Indonesia, and Brazil lack the power. Of the world's larger states, that leaves Europe, or more precisely the medium-sized powers in Western Europe—especially Britain and France but perhaps also the Federal Republic of Germany (FRG), Italy, and Benelux.

It has been argued that Europe is a nonasset in the context of a world role. McGeorge Bundy, an advisor to two Presidents, once said that nothing in his "failures of perception over the last twenty years" is more striking than his inability to "foresee the degree to which the role of Western Europe would be reduced in other continents." And he added that this renunciation of power abroad seems irreversible.

On the other hand, the exclusively European focus of these countries seems bound to change. Their very dynamics are already generating commercial, cultural, and hence political involvement in other continents. World trade grows annually at a rate two or three times the growth in world economic product, creating an even greater international interdependence in economic and fiscal matters, where the inevitable conflicts have to be resolved through the international political process. Thus, in time, Europe should again become a subject, as well as an object, of power—albeit on a far smaller scale than the superpowers, but perhaps less inhibited in its actions due to that very fact.

When Europe does emerge from the shell of postwar and postcolonial isolation, it seems important that patterns of active cooperation between Europe and the United States be maintained rather than allowed to atrophy into mutual noninvolvement. In short, a prosperous, secure, and independent Europe working with North America for common purposes seems as much a part as it ever has of the American national interest, both narrowly defined and in the larger sense of the global environment in which we all must live, if we are to live at all.

Finally, on the more pragmatic side of global politics, Europe is where American and Soviet interests have clashed, for the simple reason that the direct Soviet challenge has been posed there more than in any other area. Even the Cuban missile crisis probably was an outgrowth of the Russian push on Berlin. In an era of confrontation, the United States had to respond where challenged, in, as President Kennedy said, "the testing place of Western courage and will; if we do not meet our commitments to Berlin where will we later stand?" For some critics, this is easy to dismiss as cold war rhetoric; yet the principle is as old as international conflict itself. Pericles urged Athens to reject a Spartan ultimatum on the grounds that "this trifle is both the assurance and proof of your determination."[5] And if President Nixon's hope to enter an era of negotiation is reciprocated, then negotiations must take place in the area where the issues are, and must deal with them realistically, taking account of the stakes involved and the long-term trend of world politics.

Such "simple solutions" as parallel American and Soviet disengagement, a remote-control joint superpower condominium with respect to Europe, or a united Europe as a third force are prospects, if at all, for the 1980's. The bargaining about European security in the 1970's must be based on the realities of 1970—avoiding the Scylla of prior cold-war rigidity as well as the Charybdis of wish-thinking about the future. Revisionists and advocates of historical discontinuity must reckon that two sides, not merely one, have to change their perceptions and that the rate and direction of change needs to be at least partially symmetrical.

Eastern Europe

It is the worst kind of geographic oversimplification to lump together states as different as Poland, East Germany, Hungary, Czechoslovakia, Rumania, and Bulgaria—which of course contain a large number of divergent nationalities. In some ways it is even more artificial than similarly treating the countries of

Western Europe, for in the East there is no real sense of spontaneous community beyond the Communist Party network, economic standardization on the Soviet model, and the window dressing of the Warsaw Pact. Leadership, domestic and foreign problems, and traditions vary widely. Yet in degree, at least, these countries share a need for capital to modernize their productivity; a desire for trade, especially in consumer goods; and an inclination to achieve a modicum of independence or, at least, maneuvering room in their international political, cultural, and economic relations vis-à-vis the Soviet Union—although none of their current leadership seem to want to risk a repetition of the Czech experiment of 1968, let alone the Hungarian experience of 1956. They also share a party structure of more or less doctrinaire Marxist-Leninists and a concern about current German *Ostpolitik* stemming from experience with Hitler's version.

As a group, the East European Warsaw Pact countries probably assess the various forms of conference diplomacy and propaganda as propositions from which they can only gain—in their relationship to the West, the Soviet Union, or both—without appearing to transgress the limits of the permissible. Czechoslovakia wants to obtain settlement of certain claims and establish the invalidity of the Munich Treaty. Poland and East Germany are, of course, special cases. The former is anxious to gain formal acceptance of the Oder-Neisse borderline as its western frontier, in an attempt to preclude any future German claim to the lost territories and, perhaps, also to cut down on the extra leverage which Soviet policy has thereby in Warsaw. East Germany is ruled by the last Stalinist in Eastern Europe and continues to seek international recognition of its boundaries, its legal status, and its claim to eventual sovereignty over Berlin—as long as no change in its own status quo is involved. It also relies on access to the European Common Market by the special "interzonal" trade arrangements which it has with West Germany. And East Germany may particularly desire to confirm its role in the European scheme of things before facing the inevitable internal scramble for leadership after Ulbricht.

On balance, and in view of the situation in Eastern Europe, one can conceive of a Soviet settlement with the West, however unlikely, which would not be in accord with the interests of some other Warsaw Pact countries; but it is even harder to conceive of the reverse. Ulbricht may thus be the lowest common denominator—and even more influential thereby.

Western Europe

The Scandinavian members of NATO (Norway, Denmark, and Iceland) have long tended to be detente oriented, not only by virtue of their socialist tradition but also because this is often the most readily available outlet for the foreign policy energies of these smaller powers. There is also a pattern of neutralism in Northern Europe. Norway, which aside from Turkey has the only NATO border fronting directly on the Soviet Union, has maintained a strong vote of confidence in the NATO security system, with a majority of one hundred forty-four to six in the last Storting vote. Denmark, more sheltered from the Soviet Union but sharing the legacy of a German occupation in World War II, has tended to see NATO as a vehicle for containing Germany. Accordingly, it is receptive to other European security arrangements which would accomplish the same end.

At the southern end of the Alliance, Greece and Turkey are special cases, in terms of both internal and external politics and in view of their conflict over Cyprus. Feeling vulnerable to Soviet and satellite pressures, needing external assistance, and being geographically removed from central Europe—with the current Greek regime now additionally isolated politically—they are unlikely to play significant roles in the context of European security arrangements, although both are sensitive to and quite conservative about changes in the overall climate of East-West relations. They do not, however, wish to be left out of any future negotiations which could affect the future of Southeast Europe.

Portugal, preoccupied with African problems, is also a special case and, like Greece and Turkey, is also conservative in approach.

Canada has maintained a lively interest in international peacekeeping and in "detente." But under Prime Minister Trudeau, Canada has sought to redefine her international role, both generally and in the Alliance. A diminution of her military contribution to NATO will inevitably devalue her political weight in the European security context. But Canada is also unique—as the other North American member of NATO.

Benelux, it has been said, provides the only true Europeans; and, indeed, the leadership provided to Europe by the Belgians and Dutch has been disproportionately high. Seeking to balance the larger powers of the Six, the Benelux nations have championed Britain's application for entry into the Common Market over French objections and in many other ways have formed the nucleus of Europe. If Europe in the political sense exists at all and has a capital, it is doubtless Brussels—the seat of the three European communities, as well as NATO.

Both Belgium and Holland have been staunch members of NATO, although the former's defense efforts have on occasion proved disappointing. But both have also been in the forefront of the search for detente as well as defense; the NATO report which characterizes these objectives as the twin tasks for the future of the Alliance bears the name of Belgian Foreign Minister Harmel. Until the invasion of Czechoslovakia brought a temporary halt, both countries had engaged in bilateral talks of a broad nature with individual members of the Warsaw Pact and were seeking to activate the informal Group of Ten (three smaller nations of NATO, three Warsaw Pact members, and four European neutral countries).[6]

Before turning to the four larger powers of Western Europe, a word needs to be said about the role of the European idea. Seven or eight years ago, the belief was quite widespread that a United States of Europe was destined to spring almost full blown from the initial successes of the European Common Market. This vision by European federalists proved to have grossly "underestimated the realities of time and political geography."[7] And so did the Americans who feared a rival inward-looking European bloc, as well as those who sought a transatlantic partnership of equals, in the expectation, perhaps, that the European partner could assume responsibility for its own defense.

The ideal, however, had enough political appeal that General de Gaulle found it necessary twice to veto British membership and thus to defer the emergence of a rival to his own concept of a Europe, in which the leading role would be played by France. If current British negotiations with the Common Market prove successful, then the federalist dream may again acquire momentum. Meanwhile, for the next several years at least, a European entity with disposative powers over resources and with a common foreign and defense policy is not in the cards—nor is a Europe with modern military power sufficient to counterbalance Russian pressure without continued American commitments and the deployments which make them credible.

Nevertheless, however deferred and uncertain it may be, the very prospect of a European entity of major significance is surely a factor—and one viewed with mixed feelings—in the foreign policies of the Soviet Union and Eastern Europe. This prospect may provide some additional rationale for an attempt to settle outstanding East-West issues—particularly those involving Germany— sooner rather than later. At the same time, it must also increase the Soviet incentive to to divide the Western Europeans from each other and from the United States. For the possible relationships between the "little" Europe of the Six and a wider Europe, extending to the Vistula if not to the Urals, have never emerged clearly.

Germany

The problem of competing identities—between the Atlantic alliance, Western European unity, and reunification with Eastern Europe—is felt most sharply in divided Germany. The Social Democrat and Free Democrat left-center coalition seems to be cautiously feeling its way toward a possible accommodation with East Germany and perhaps an eventual settlement with the Soviet Union. Chancellor Brandt's *Ostpolitik* is also oriented toward penetrating the markets of Eastern Europe as an outlet for the West German capital surplus. Depending on its outcome, this might permit a genuine long-term settlement of the problems of Germany and Berlin to emerge on a pragmatic basis. The proclaimed Western goal of German reunification on the basis of free elections has always seemed unrealistic. Quite apart from the Soviet Union's unyielding opposition, no other West European country really wishes to see East Germany's twenty million people and thirty billion dollar gross national product added to a Federal Republic which already outstrips its neighbors on both counts. Estimates differ on how strongly a majority of Germans, especially the younger generations, feel about reunification. But it is too good a political issue not to become a lively point of contention at whatever moment seems most propitious to the opposition, given the current coalition's precarious majority.

The Socialist dilemma is that they were scarred once in the days of the Weimar Republic by the charge of selling out to Germany's enemies. Emotional charges, such as abandonment of the unification goal by virtue of recognizing East Germany, could easily be raised again. The result might be a reaction of uncertain scope but one bound to be unsettling to all of Germany's neighbors. (Indeed, more than one observer has speculated that the Soviet Union can acquire increased control over Brandt's political destiny by protracted negotiations, or as one put it somewhat crudely, by the possibility of coitus interruptus. In some respects it can be argued that the Soviets would be more comfortable with a Bonn regime which again could be described as revanchist and dangerous, because Germanophobia gives Russia increased leverage over Eastern Europe.)

The Germans themselves are doubtless aware of the dangers, and Chancellor Brandt has been at some pains to emphasize, for both foreign and domestic consumption, the priority his government places, in declaratory policy at least, on a strong Western alliance.[8] The other dilemma—that between European and Atlantic policies, which involves West Germany's need for close ties with both Paris and Washington—has been quietly eased by the departure of General de Gaulle.

Great Britain

Under the Wilson government, Great Britain has also reduced the pressure of one horn of its traditional dilemma between Europe and the world; although the special relationship with Washington remains, in muted form, Britain's withdrawal from East of Suez has permitted an overtly European policy, centered on the Common Market. But British politics at home have placed a considerable premium on East-West contacts and negotiations. Britain's wartime role and special responsibilities in Berlin guarantee that the United Kingdom will be a major actor in the stage of European security—albeit one susceptible to trade blandishments and prone to "looking on the bright side," even at the expense of realism in evaluating the prospects. Britain has expressed interest in a series of conferences to explore European security issues,[9] and she has been ardent in pursuit of various arms control measures. On the other hand, Defense Minister Healey has increased Britain's defense spending for 1970 and sought leadership in a European caucus on defense matters.

France

"Gaullism without de Gaulle" appears to be in transition. Some of the sharper clashes of French nationalism with her European partners, with the United States, and with NATO have been muted, and so have the *son et lumière* characteristics of a Franco-Russian rapprochement. But opposition to anything smacking of bloc-to-bloc diplomacy is still manifested by the Elysée and the Quai, which complicates NATO's necessary coordinating role in Western diplomacy. As a member of the quadripartite group on Berlin, however, France has been disposed to be somewhat more cooperative.

French policy could take one (or more) of several directions: leadership in detente overtures—largely, as before, for reasons of domestic politics or special trade opportunities, but perhaps also with an element of historical reversion to France's interwar policy of alliance with Eastern Europe to contain Germany; concentration on rebuilding the Paris-Bonn special relationship; establishment of a modus vivendi or even a tacit partnership with Britain; continuation in the role of playing an increasingly lone hand, of the type recently in evidence in French dealings with the Arab world, especially on arms. In any case, France, along with Britain and Germany, will ensure that it remains a major actor in the European security drama.

Italy

Italy has relatively few indigenous foreign policy issues; the conflict with Yugoslavia over Trieste being long past and that with Austria over the Alto Aldige being nearly so. But the Italians have a tradition of *presenza,* of wanting to be a participant in diplomatic activities of all types, irrespective of their inclination or ability to make a substantive contribution. This is compounded by an internal crisis that many observers believe to be of major, some even say revolutionary, proportions. The traditional allegiances of the Italian electorate tend to be tied either to parties with international affiliations, for example, the Communists (with Moscow- and Peking-oriented factions) or Socialists, or to politico-economic-religious groupings, which do not normally build their planks out of the pragmatic issues that the country faces at home. This gives domestic politics an unusually facile springboard into international politics and vice versa. One can expect Italian leaders, therefore, to embrace "openings to the left" in European detente politics as well as in the domestic variety and to restrain themselves only with difficulty from pursuing international appearances at the expense of reality.

The Neutrals

The major European countries who are not members either of NATO or the Warsaw Pact are Austria, Finland, Spain, Sweden, Switzerland, and Yugoslavia. Sweden and Switzerland are neutrals by tradition, and traders with all comers by necessity. Neither is likely to be directly affected by or particularly influenced on the major European security issues. Finland, neutral by force of its World War II peace treaty, is independent and a member of the Nordic Council, but in some ways she is also a de facto protectorate of the Soviet Union. In May 1969, the Finnish government sent a memorandum to thirty-two governments, offering to act as host for an East-West European security conference. According to its spokesman, this was a completely independent initiative, taken because of Finland's role as a small neutral country and out of a sense of responsibility for "the peaceful development of Europe."[10] It is worth noting that the preliminary sessions of the Soviet-American strategic arms limitation talks (SALT) were held in Helsinki in December 1969. The second phase is scheduled for April 1970 in Vienna—a capital which has also stressed its role as a bridge between East and West. President Kennedy's 1961 meeting with Khrushchev took place there, and the Austrians have continued to seek an international role commensurate with their "permanent neutrality" status—perhaps to keep alive at least a glimmer of the diplomatic glory of the Hapsburgs.

Spain, which has a special agreement with the Common Market and belongs to the Organization for Economic Cooperation and Development (OECD), is a natural member of the Western community, with historic ties to the New World as well as the Old. Yet efforts to bring about Spanish membership in NATO have been frustrated by opposition of several countries, especially those with Socialist governments whose leaders first earned their political spurs against Franco in the Spanish Civil War. Spain is not involved (other than ideologically) on East-West issues; but it is hard to envisage a long-term European security arrangement which does not include all of the Iberian Peninsula, since in the long run Europe and Spain need each other. Perhaps this can be accomplished as part of the transition following the Franco regime.

Yugoslavia is the first, and only successful, defector from Soviet control. She has sought an international role among the world's nonaligned but would be potentially involved in any European security settlement, as a World War II belligerent and by reasons of geography. Whether or not Yugoslavia could perform any role as a mediator is more doubtful. Although neutral, she is still regarded as a renegade by the orthodox members of the Warsaw Pact.

Other Interested Countries

Juridically speaking, the European security issues of 1970 are primarily unfinished business from World War II, although their substance is largely of cold war origin. Thus, any international negotiations which purport to settle the German question, whether designed as or in lieu of a peace treaty, could theoretically involve the potential interests, or at least claims for representation, of some nineteen Latin American countries who were nominal belligerents, plus Egypt, Ethopia, Iraq, and the major non-European allies, such as China, India, Australia, and South Africa. Counting NATO and the Warsaw Pact and certain neutrals, this totals nearly fifty countries! There would doubtless have to be a link to the United Nations; and the pressures for representation could easily dwarf those which led to the expansion of the (currently) Eighteen Nation Disarmament Conference at Geneva. It is a settled rule of diplomacy that the number claiming to be heard (or at least seen) in a major international conference setting bears an inverse relationship to their actual interests and ability to contribute. *Presenza* is an Italian word but a human failing.

3 The Evolution of Security Diplomacy

The newest Russian invitation to discuss the issues which divide the Continent reminds many observers of the recurring pattern of postwar crises, conferences, and maneuvering; so that the recent series of Soviet proposals for a European security conference is often regarded with a sense of déja vu.

On the other hand, this new appeal to "progressive and peace-loving forces" inevitably strikes a responsive chord in the citizens of America and Europe who pay the bills for maintaining the military forces to balance the large standing Soviet military capability, even though the conference idea does not yet appear to have become a major public issue in the West. In addition to the sensible approach to problem solving which conference diplomacy implies to the layman, he recalls from history that Waterloo and the Marne were followed by Vienna and Versailles. Soviet efforts to convene "a peace conference to mark the end of World War II" seem to be the long-delayed sequel to Stalingrad and Normandy.[1]

The Communist approach grows quite naturally out of a history of party congresses and ideological conclaves, such as those which have traditionally assembled workers, intellectuals, and other "progressive elements" in the three Internationals, in the soviets themselves, and in the public gatherings which are preferred for demonstrating solidarity in the struggle against capitalism and imperialism.

From the initial session of the First International in London in 1864 to the Conference of Communist and Workers' Parties in Moscow in June 1969,

Communists have preferred to appear to conduct their politics within the conference framework, in order to inspire the faithful and ratify the decisions already made by the few who comprise the "revolutionary vanguard" and determine the "correct line." Conferences are thus major events of historical consequence, where difficult problems are solved dialectically and new directions are charted. Aside from these psychopolitical aspects of Communist "conferencemanship," considerations of international status are involved in attending a major conference and in shaping diplomatic events—especially where the subject of discussion is Europe's future. In that regard, the Soviet proposal for a new East-West conference on European security is related to the origins and modern trends of Russian diplomacy toward the West.

Interwar Russian Diplomacy

The diplomatic objectives of the last Czarist government were to hasten the disintegration of the Turkish and Hapsburg empires, to weaken the German dynasty and extend Russian influence by the annexation of certain portions of Poland and Prussia, to gain access to the Mediterranean through the Turkish straits and to achieve the partition of Austria-Hungary. To some extent, at least, Russia's World War I allies encouraged those parts of this program which would weaken Germany. But the Revolution sharply curtailed Russian diplomatic goals to little more than discouraging foreign interference in the internal convulsions during four years of civil war. In the process, the Soviet Union experienced its first military defeat, at the hands of Poland in 1920-1921, and lost territories and population to the states of Eastern Europe. This setback and the allied interventions in the civil war were seen as confirmation that the imperialists would inevitably take advantage of Russian weakness.

Viewed in this perspective, the League of Nations amounted to little more than an alliance of capitalist powers aimed at further weakening and isolating the new Marxist state. Resistance to such encirclement demanded a rapid internal consolidation of power and planning for the international extension of Soviet objectives, for reasons of external security and ideological necessity. This decision was reflected in Lenin's triumph over Trotsky's thesis of permanent revolution.

Rapallo and Locarno

Central to the twin objectives of maintaining a defensive diplomatic posture, albeit with a strident propaganda facade, and advancing the world revolution was the concentration of subversive activities in postwar Germany. In the ideological tradition of Marxism-Leninism, the industrial proletariat of Germany was the prime target for revolutionary mobilizations. And even though the Weimar Republic withstood the Comintern, the German Communist Party was the largest nonruling Communist Party in Europe until it was extinguished by the rise of National Socialism. The Soviet failure to generate a successful revolution in Germany coincided with consolidation at home, the building of socialism in Russia, and a somewhat more conventional diplomacy abroad. In the latter case, the initial achievement of Soviet diplomacy was the Rapallo Treaty with Germany in 1922.[2]

Today, as commentators evaluate Willy Brandt's *Ostpolitik* and Soviet willingness to enter bilateral negotiations with West Germany for economic benefits and mutual renunciation of force, there are frequent references to another Rapallo. Rapallo was indeed greeted with indignation by Britain and France, but this Russo-German bilateral agreement of the 1920's involved a different power relationship between the parties than is the case now, nearly fifty years later. For the international power position of the Soviet Union was extremely weak in 1922. As the date of the world revolution continued to be postponed in the wake of seven years of fighting at home and abroad, the Russian leadership reviewed with alarm the drastic condition of the Russian economy, which urgently demanded restoration for the sake of Soviet security as the platform from which later efforts would be launched toward world revolution.

By agreement with the Germans in 1922, the Red Army and the Russian economy were strengthened by German credit and technical assistance. Germany and the Soviet Union did not form a military alliance, yet the Russian leadership was partially and temporarily reassured by Rapallo that the recovering might of Germany was not being marshaled in an aggressive anti-Soviet posture led by the "league of capitalists." The agreement also aided the post-World War I diplomatic recovery of Germany. And it followed the nineteenth-century tradition of Bismarck, who thought benevolent relations with Russia were essential to his maneuvering powers in order to maintain a delicate balance of alignments. Recognizing the tendency of this rapprochement, the Western powers, particularly Britain, appealed to German desires for expanded international legitimacy and encouraged the series of diplomatic exchanges which concluded in the so-called Locarno treaties in 1925. The Soviets reacted harshly to these efforts, which they interpreted as consolidating an anti-Communist western front or at least limiting German reliability for Soviet security interests.

Just as an impulsive Kaiser changed the basis of European security and Russo-German relations before World War I, the rise of Hitler and German National Socialism brought an evaporation of the Locarno spirit of collective security and a reversal of Russian diplomatic posture. At first, this posture moved toward the alternative to entente with Germany—namely, a resumption of beneficial relations with France and a more active interest in the League of Nations. But when German rearmament went unopposed and the Western powers failed to act in the face of fascist advances in Ethiopia, Spain, and Manchuria, the Soviet leadership reevaluated the implications for Russian security—particularly in light of Hitler's ambitions in east and southeast Europe.

Accordingly, one can understand why Stalin viewed the Munich agreement as demonstrating Western willingness to redirect the aggressive aspirations of Nazi Germany eastward toward Soviet borders. The result was the maneuvering which led to a fourth partition of Poland and the Nazi-Soviet nonaggression pact of August 1939—a division of central Europe into Soviet and Nazi spheres of influence, accompanied by, in effect, a mutual renunciation of force. It proved to be short lived, lasting only until the Germans invaded Russia on June 22, 1941.

In summary, the record of interwar diplomacy illustrates the tendency of states to utilize conferences, treaties, and political guarantees of collective security in the face of difficult choices in balance-of-power and deterrence diplomacy.

Early Postwar Diplomacy

It has been noted that World War II brought a new distribution of power in Europe, and accordingly the European security problem assumed new proportions:

> The result of the war was to bring into preeminence the two great continental powers, the Soviet Union and the United States, and to place these two super-powers in a position of proximity which they might otherwise never have known. Between them lay Germany, and by that fact alone—far more than by its defeat—Germany acquired a totally different aspect. Germany became in fact like Poland of the eighteenth century, and its partition was equally inevitable. Germany united on either side of the new balance of power would destroy the balance; while an independent middle power would be a constant threat to its neighbors on each side.[3]

The substance of the German problem—including Berlin—as the dominant issue of European security is reviewed in greater detail in the next chapter. What is of special interest here, however, is the role of conference politics in cold war diplomacy and the various peace plans which have marked the postwar debate over the future of Europe.

Russian diplomacy since 1945 has been a mixture of threats and promises, inducements and harassments—a panoply of tactics which have ranged from Khrushchev's threats to incinerate the Acropolis and to forcibly remove the

Berlin "bone" from his throat to the euphoric spirit of Geneva and of Camp David, to shoe-pounding exercises at the United Nations and "controlled hysteria" after the abortive 1960 summit meeting. The Berlin Wall has been opened during the Christmas season, yet periodic harassment of the access routes to Berlin has continued into 1970. Soviet tactics to achieve their foreign policy goals in Europe have included the use of trade blandishments, general strikes by Communist workers in Western Europe, and threats of nuclear blackmail.

But there has also been the conference strategy, with which the Western allies first became familiar in the negotiations during and after World War II. The summit meetings at Yalta and Potsdam established the machinery for the temporary government of Germany—the four-power Allied Control Council and the Reparations Commission.[4] During the next two years, the major questions of European security were discussed in the repeated sessions of the four-power Council of Foreign Ministers. One of the first items they considered was a proposal for a twenty-five year four-power guarantee treaty against the recurrence of German aggression. The provisions of this plan called for the complete neutralization and demilitarization of a reunified Germany. At Soviet request, the Western allies agreed to extend the term of the proposed treaty to forty years, and in the meetings of the Ministers during the spring and fall of 1947, Secretary Marshall pushed for its acceptance. But Molotov's opposition brought failure to the negotiations in the context of a general hardening of Soviet policy.[5]

A new meeting of the four-power Foreign Ministers took place at the end of the Berlin blockade. At that meeting Secretary Acheson called for the reunification of Germany on the basis of four-power control. But the withdrawal of occupation forces was unacceptable to the Soviet Union, and by the fall of 1949 two German republics were established, constituting the status quo for the next two decades.

During 1950 and 1951, conference politics gave way to Western preoccupation over Korea and the buildup of Western defenses in NATO. The Soviets countered the growing West German military integration with Western Europe by a diplomatic offensive initiated on March 10, 1952, with the proclamation of a Soviet outline of the foundations for a German peace treaty. This démarche went the farthest of any yet seen, calling for German reunification on the basis of neutralization and the mutual withdrawal of foreign troops and bases. But the most daring innovation was its direct appeal to German national sentiments.

According to the Soviet plan, Germany would "be allowed to have national land, air, and sea forces essential to the defense of the country," without restrictions on the production of armaments for those forces.

Furthermore, and as a major attraction to veterans, all former members of the German army and former Nazis would be granted "civil and political rights on a par with all other German citizens to participate in building a peace-loving and democratic Germany." And finally, German membership in the United Nations was to be supported by states signing the peace treaty.[6]

These concessions—remarkable when compared with the preceding Soviet attitudes—were aimed at devaluing the Western call for German rearmament within an integrated European army. Meanwhile, the Russian initiative also appealed to fears of Germany as well as to the inclinations of those who wanted to "solve" the German problem. To Germans it offered reunification without the indignities of international control, as well as the restoration of national forces as a major attribute of sovereignty.

The Soviet note of 1952 opened a three-year offensive aimed at preventing or delaying the consolidation of the Western defensive position on the basis of German rearmament. The Russian omnibus proposal was greeted coolly in the West: Chancellor Adenauer declined to accept neutralization and the loss of Germany's eastern territories. Western Europeans saw endangered their budding efforts to build a united Europe which included the critical West German economy. And Americans, concerned with a global Communist threat, had been counting on a West German military contribution. The Western reply took the form of a call for free elections supervised by a commission from the United Nations, with which the East refused to treat at all.

One year later, the death of Stalin sparked renewed interest by the Western allies in probing the attitudes of the new Soviet leadership about European issues. This led to a Western proposal in late 1953 for a four-power conference on Germany, against the background of an "agonizing reappraisal" of American foreign policy if the proposed European Defense Community fell through. The outcome of these developments was a new meeting of the Council of Foreign Ministers which was held in Berlin in January 1954.

The First Eden Plan

At the January 1954 conference, the British Foreign Secretary, Sir Anthony Eden, proposed what has since been called the First Eden Plan for German reunification—a five-stage proposal, to be initiated by free elections throughout Germany. The reunified state would be given full sovereignty regarding acceptance or rejection of future diplomatic and military alignments. Yet it was apparent from the premises of the proposal that such a reunited state would incline toward partnership with the West. This, of course, made Soviet rejection inevitable. But in order to avoid the onus for failure at the Berlin conference, Molotov offered the "Soviet proposal of European security," which, in effect, added a fifty-year collective security pact to the Soviet treaty outline of March 1952. Since they were by then fully committed to the objective of free elections in Germany, the Western powers were unable to agree to the enforced limitations of self-determination which were implied by Soviet demands for a neutral Germany.

After the final failure of Soviet policy to prevent West German integration with the West, represented by the special NATO-Western European Union accords in London and Paris in the fall of 1954, the Russians opened a new spring offensive. This called, for the first time, for the withdrawal of Soviet troops from Poland, as well as mutual force reductions in Germany. And on the eve of the Federal Republic's official entry into NATO, the Soviet Union recommended "free, all-German elections in accordance with the Eden Plan." But, in his final appearance as Prime Minister, Malenkov also threatened countermeasures if Germany entered NATO. And the countermeasures proved to be the establishment of the Warsaw Pact less than a week after the formal admission of the Federal Republic to the Western alliance.

The Geneva Summit

Reassured by this diplomatic defeat of the Soviet political offensive, the West moved to negotiate from strength. The meeting took place in Geneva in mid-1955—just a decade after the last summit meeting—and this assembly of the four-power heads of government had important implications for the next ten to fifteen years of European politics. Eden, then Prime Minister of Great Britain, offered his second plan, a proposal which called for a demilitarized area between East and West on the eastern frontier of Germany as "a practical experiment in the operative control of armaments." Eden continued to insist that a reunified Germany have the "freedom to associate with countries of her choice." But since "the Berlin Conference failed . . . because one of the Powers there believed that a united Germany, rearmed and exercising its choice to join the NATO alliance, would constitute an increased threat to its safety and security," Eden proposed a security pact.

Speaking for the Soviet side, Marshal Bulganin picked up the idea of a collective security pact and advocated it as a replacement for NATO and the Warsaw Treaty Organization. And in a theme which relates directly to the current Soviet proposals for a European security conference, Bulganin spoke of a mutual renunciation of force as well as a freeze on existing levels of armed forces.

In addition, he called for the "withdrawal of foreign troops from the territories of European states and the reestablishment of the situation which existed prior to the Second World War," namely, the unilateral withdrawal of American forces from Europe. Finally, he emphasized a new and growing theme in Soviet diplomatic pronouncements—one now familiar to observers of current events in Germany—the necessity of a rapprochement between the two parts of Germany.

The product of the Geneva summit meeting was the "Directive of the Heads of Governments to Their Foreign Ministers," requesting the examination of these major items: a security pact for Europe or for part of Europe; limitations, control, and inspection of armaments and armed forces; the establishment between East and West of a zone in which the disposition of armed forces would be subject to mutual agreement; and an all-German council to deal with matters of free elections and German political development.

These proposals are important, for they foretold the proliferation of disengagement plans and arms-limitation-zone schemes, which reached their high watermark in the late 1950's. Furthermore, the Geneva summit marked a major turning point in postwar diplomacy—some writers have even called it the "Versailles of the Cold War."[7] From these meetings there emerged the main lines of mutually opposing East-West policies which persisted for the next fifteen years.

For the East this took the form of the familiar policy of "two Germanies," based on a consolidation of the Communist position in the German Democratic Republic. The doctrine of two Germanies now involved a Soviet recognition of the status quo by the extension of diplomatic recognition to the Federal Republic and an invitation to its Chancellor to visit Moscow. Since 1955, Russian diplomacy has consistently demanded reciprocal gestures from the West—diplomatic recognition of the German Democratic Republic and acceptance of the impossibility of finding a mutually acceptable alternative to German partition.

For its part, the West adopted an equal and opposite reaction to the Soviet stand. Under the firm policy of Adenauer and Dulles, NATO declined to recognize the legitimacy of the GDR or to acknowledge the de facto existence of a divided Europe with mutually exclusive spheres of control. However, in an unusual preview of the *Ostpolitik* of today, Secretary Dulles said in 1955:

> The problem of German reunification can be solved at present only gradually, step by step, through bringing closer together the German Democratic Republic and the German Federal Republic and through their co-operation.[8]

Not surprisingly, the Council of Foreign Ministers struggled vainly to reach agreement on the issues given them by the Geneva summit directive. The Soviets raised the price of troop withdrawals from East Germany by demanding withdrawals from the territories of European countries. And Molotov demanded an all-German council as the alternative to free elections.

However, the proposal for a zone of controlled armaments—a Geneva agenda item largely avoided by the Foreign Ministers in late 1955—whetted the imaginations of a number of commentators. During 1955 through 1958, there were numerous variants to the disengagement thesis of Eden's second plan. And regional arms-control measures were discussed in the United Nations Disarmament Commission. There were private plans and official proposals that called for mutual force reductions, zones of inspection, exchanges of observers, observation posts, and the dismantling of foreign bases. Furthermore, there were several efforts to reduce the risks of miscalculations, such as the proposals for safeguards against surprise attack.[9]

By the fall of 1957 there was increasing interest in a much publicized suggestion of the Polish Foreign Minister. The Rapacki Plan called for a denuclearized zone in central Europe, and a simultaneous reduction of forces in both Germanies, as well as in Poland and Czechoslovakia. Similarly, the Reith lectures of George Kennan and the publications of Denis Healey called for reunification based on withdrawal of foreign troops from Central Europe, restraints on united Germany's arms and political orientation, and a European security pact as part of a guarantee by the superpowers. The Soviet Union joined in this call for disengagement and repeated the appeal for the signing of a nonaggression pact between NATO and the Warsaw Treaty Organization. Many of these ideas of the 1950's have been recycled through the literature of the 1960's, especially by some of the revisionist and anti-establishment writers, who rarely seem to concern themselves with the reasons why all the ideas have proved unworkable in practice.[10]

The Berlin Crisis

As the debate over disengagement proceeded through 1958, there was little indication that the Russian leadership was preparing to reopen the Berlin question until the famous Soviet ultimatum of Thanksgiving Day in November 1958. Khrushchev's demand for troop withdrawal, demilitarization, and neutralization was confined to only one zone—West Berlin. The quid pro quo which he offered consisted solely of relinquishment of Russian occupation rights in East Germany. Perhaps the Russians were trying to impress upon the peoples of Eastern Europe the "fact" of permanent Communist rule and the necessity to "build socialism," and thereby discourage new uprisings such as those which had occurred in East Berlin, Poznan, and Budapest. Nevertheless, the key to this objective was the need to shore up Russia's weak German client by two means: the acceptance by the West of the Soviet policy of two Germanies, to be demonstrated by formal Western diplomatic recognition of the GDR; and Western cooperation in the sealing off of Berlin as the point of escape for the youthful, highly skilled workers from East Germany.

The previous enthusiasm for disengagement plans and neutral belts in Europe faded as Soviet pressure intensified during the second Berlin crisis. However, a number of proposals endorsed Khrushchev's "free-city" idea and related it to such schemes as the transfer of the United Nations headquarters from New York to Berlin. In their rejection of the Soviet ultimatum, the Western powers expressed a willingness to negotiate about Germany's future, but not under duress. Within two weeks Russia replied with a new version of its draft German peace treaty, along with the old demands for foreign-troop withdrawal, German renunciation of nuclear weapons, recognition of current territorial borders, and a neutral united Germany. Then, on the occasion of NATO's tenth anniversary, the Soviet Union repeated the proposal for a nonaggression pact between NATO and the Warsaw Treaty members. Shortly thereafter, the four-power Council of Foreign Ministers resumed talks after an interlude of nearly four years.

Geneva Revisited

At the Geneva meetings of foreign ministers in mid-1959, Secretary of State Herter amalgamated the previous Western proposals (mainly those from the two Eden plans) into a "Western Peace Plan," which softened some aspects of the provisions concerning a mixed German committee yet maintained the demand that a future all-German government must have freedom of choice in military alignments. The Soviet reaction took the form of a number of speeches by Khrushchev during the summer and fall of 1959. His principal declaration took place in an address to the United Nations General Assembly, following his meetings with President Eisenhower at Camp David. Khrushchev reiterated the Soviet policy on foreign troops in Europe and the need for an atom-free zone in central Europe. His emphasis, however, lay in the drive for "general and complete disarmament." Hence, the ultimatum on Berlin faded into a grandiose scheme for world disarmament and a trip to the ill-fated summit of 1960.

Nevertheless, the concentration on Berlin as the target for Soviet policy aims in East Germany and East Europe did establish the belief in many minds that the Berlin situation was indeed an "abnormality." The flood of refugees continued through the free city, and the psychological and economic effects, against which the 1958 ultimatum was directed, not only remained but also were intensified as tensions mounted in Europe.

Khrushchev raised the issue again as he tested the will of newly elected President Kennedy in Vienna in 1961. But the "final solution" to the second Berlin crisis occurred with the construction of the Berlin Wall on August 13, 1961. Some commentators add an epilogue to this chapter in the history of the Berlin question by linking the Cuban missile crisis of October 1962. In retrospect, it seems probable that Khrushchev's Cuban gamble was related to a desire to obtain political leverage on the German problem by a publicized shift in the strategic balance.[11]

Incidents on the access routes took place in 1963 and 1964, reminding the West that the Berlin issue was still warm, albeit on the back burner. Yet the high point of tension in the diplomacy of European security had been passed, at least insofar as the era of bold plans and conference politics.

In reviewing this period, one author observes that American spokesmen during the Kennedy years emphasized:

> The only sensible course was to accept the division as an enforced reality, which only war could undo, and encourage increased contacts with the eastern zone to better the lot and maintain the hopes of those denied their political rights by the Soviet system . . . . No agreement remotely satisfactory was possible, none was really even necessary, since the situation was finally stable if admittedly imperfect.[12]

The Gaullist Initiative

Political observers in the mid-1960's spoke of "small steps," and West Germany cautiously edged toward a "policy of movement." But the most dramatic initiatives were made by the President of France—moves which were symbolized and accentuated in 1966 by France's withdrawal from the military side of NATO and de Gaulle's visit to Moscow.

Curiously enough, the de Gaulle visit proved to be the high point of the brief Franco-Russian "affair," and grandiose projects of technological and space cooperation dwindled away in their execution. Apparently, the Soviets found de Gaulle useful up to a point but were unwilling to treat with him on major security issues, where he lacked the power "to do business." This implied a devaluation of French grandeur that could hardly have been pleasing to the General.

The sequence and substance of the Gaullist approach seems related to the current Soviet call for a conference on European security; for in a February 1965 press conference, President de Gaulle noted:

> . . . this matter will not be settled by the direct confrontation of ideologies and forces of the two camps . . . . What must be done will

not be done, one day, except by the understanding and combined action of the peoples who have always been, who are, and who will remain principally concerned by the fate of the German neighbor—in short, the European peoples.[13]

In this program to "make a new equilibrium possible on our continent," de Gaulle appealed to national sentiments, East and West, even those "satellitized" by the Soviet Union.

French efforts to loosen up the European political environment occurred at a time when the leadership of the Soviet Union was less imaginative, dramatic, or perhaps not even as confidently installed in power as Khrushchev. These efforts also occurred at a time when the two superpowers were preoccupied with their respective Asian problems. Nevertheless, the European security issues, which had remained largely dormant for nearly five years gradually began to resume importance in East-West politics.

In March 1966—just at the time of the Gaullist initiatives in France, the formation of the Grand Coalition in the Federal Republic, and the deepening involvement of the United States in Vietnam—three events occurred to highlight the new crescendo. First, de Gaulle formally ended French participation in the integrated defense system of NATO. Second, the West German Grand Coalition extended a "peace note" to the East European countries, calling for a series of bilateral and mutual renunciations of force.[14] And finally, the Twenty-third Congress of the Communist Party of the Soviet Union made a general proposal for a European security conference.[15]

Speaking on behalf of the Central Committee, Party leader Brezhnev called for

negotiations on matters of European security . . . [to include] the development of peaceful, mutually advantageous ties among all European states . . . [in] an appropriate international conference.

Foreign Minister Gromyko picked up the theme of superpower prevention of the just national aspirations of Europeans and imperialist intervention in European affairs; yet, as might have been expected, he stressed only one side of that Gaullist theme (as well as agreeing with the General's geographic definition of "Europe") when he condemned "the influence wielded by a large non-European power." Hence, the conference idea was frankly aimed at appealing to "pan-European resentment" of America's military presence.

From Bucharest to Karlovy Vary

The anti-intervention theme was repeated in a statement by the political leaders of the seven active members of the Warsaw Pact, following a meeting in Bucharest in July 1966. (See Appendix C.) In deference to the hosts, however, the "Declaration on Strengthening Peace and Security in Europe" stressed an Eastern Europe interest in "noninterference in internal affairs." By calling for the simultaneous liquidation of military organizations, the Rumanians at the conference implied a curtailment of Soviet military activities in Eastern Europe. In its pan-European appeal, the Bucharest statement emphasized a broadening of the anti-American front in order to encourage "neutral European countries . . . [to] play a positive role in the convocation of such a conference." Furthermore, nonmilitary cooperation was suggested in a plea for an increase in European-wide scientific, technological, and cultural relations and in the idea that the European Common Market should be replaced by all-European trade arrangements.

Anti-West German themes, familiar in Soviet rhetoric of the 1950's, returned in the form of demands for formal recognition of the Soviet Union's two-Germanies policy—diplomatic and territorial recognition in talks with the GDR, renunciation of force (although there was no direct response to the Federal Republic's peace note issued only four months earlier), and disavowal of nuclear arms (with no acknowledgment of West Germany's 1954 self-prohibition or emphasis on the nonproliferation treaty, then under discussion). Although hopeful that West Germany's new Grand Coalition would show more flexibility and movement toward acceptance of the GDR, the Soviet leadership apparently joined East German leader Ulbricht in suspicions that West Germany's trade and credit policies with the East would undermine the "solidarity of the antifascist socialist camp." particularly in the GDR, as they had tended to do in the 1950's.

The next round in conference politics came as an Eastern reaction to the "bridge-building" policy of the United States and the *Ostpolitik* of the Federal Republic, which, by then, had established diplomatic relations with Rumania. Following the signature of a series of bilateral treaties with the GDR (not only to shore up Ulbricht once again but also, perhaps, in anticipation of the distant possibility of mutual pact dissolution), the Warsaw Pact nations sent Party representatives to the Czech spa of Karlovy Vary for a meeting in April of 1967. The Rumanians, doubtless feeling themselves in line for some Party discipline, stayed home.

This conference was somewhat pan-European as well as pan-Communist, in that sixteen Communist parties from East and West Europe attended. Acting again on the Gaullist premise that Europe should settle its own affairs, the conferees agreed to mobilize mass support in Europe to dissolve NATO (though not the Warsaw Pact as well)* and accelerate American troop

---

*The Preamble to the Warsaw Treaty of Friendship, Cooperation, and Mutual Assistance states that the parties reaffirm "their desire for the establishment of a system of European collective security based on the participation of all European states

withdrawal (with no mention of Russian garrisons in Eastern Europe). In so doing, the Russians "corrected" the notion in the Bucharest statement that troop withdrawals applied to all armed forces; only foreign troops were stipulated, recalling the earlier definition of "Europe" and thereby exempting Soviet forces in Eastern Europe.

The Karlovy Vary communique (see Appendix C) widened the call of the Bucharest statement for a conference of European states to an appeal for "a congress of the peoples of Europe on the broadest popular basis." By broadening the appeal to include Europe's social democrats, the Soviet Union hoped to quicken the socialist transformation of Western Europe on the basis of "peaceful coexistence between states of different social systems." In Brezhnev's view, detente politics would serve progressive purposes; he declared, ". . . in conditions of relaxed international tensions the arrow of the political barometer moves to the left." The events of 1968 were to prove that Brezhnev was looking at his barometer without regard to its accurate indications of change in Eastern Europe.

While NATO brought a variety of bilateral diplomatic efforts at detente into multilateral harness by way of the Harmel exercise (named for the Belgian Foreign Minister but reflecting Alliance agreement), which was followed in mid-1968 by NATO's proposal for mutual and balanced force reductions in Europe (see Appendix B)—the Soviet Union watched with increasing alarm as the pace of liberalization quickened in Czechoslovakia. The change of American policy in Vietnam and the June 1967 war in the Middle East led to the "mini-summit" at Glassboro in July 1967 and tentative plans for strategic arms limitation talks (SALT). But the necessity for a Soviet invasion as a police action in Prague and the promulgation of the Brezhnev Doctrine of "limited sovereignty" within the Communist camp, placed Soviet diplomacy on the defensive.

The Budapest Appeal

The "Message from the Warsaw Pact States to All European Countries," following a meeting in Budapest in March 1969 (see Appendix C), attempted to divert attention from the Eastern aspect of the European security problem, including the increasingly serious issue of Sino-Soviet relations. Although the tone was less polemical than previous statements, the meeting's communique

---

irrespective of their social and political systems." Article 11 provides for automatic dissolution of the Warsaw Pact when such a general European system enters into force. While this automaticity is doubtful and the Soviet Union has an extensive network of bilateral treaties in Eastern Europe anyway, this provision seems worth bearing in mind; for it is an important element in the Soviet propaganda drive for "dissolution of blocs."

was once again focused on pressure for American troop withdrawals, West German recognition of the two-Germanies program, including the dissociation of Bonn from West Berlin, and the convocation of a general European conference to discuss problems of European security and peaceful cooperation. The anti-American focus was probably linked to the rising domestic demand in the United States for withdrawal from Vietnam and "the urgent necessity to reorder America's national priorities," meaning contraction of American foreign commitments and increased action on domestic problems. The anti-German aspect of the Budapest appeal was no doubt related to the oncoming West German election campaign. In both instances the goal was to encourage European nationalism toward a more neutralist (that is, anti-American and, if possible, pro-Soviet) position in East-West relations.

Following the twentieth anniversary meeting of NATO in Washington in April 1969, the Soviet Union succeeded in obtaining neutral sponsorship for the conference. Finland sent a memorandum to all European states and to the United States and Canada calling for an assembly in early 1970. Statements by Soviet officials during mid-1969 repeated their emphasis on "a common front against imperialism," to be expressed in "a broad congress of European peoples." And Brezhnev outlined the Soviet objective that this policy should be carried out by the creation of collective security systems in Europe and Asia.

Meanwhile, the next major development in the fast-moving European security problem came as part of the formation of a left-center coalition in West Germany in October 1969. Chancellor Brandt's *Ostpolitik* was enunciated in his policy statement of October 28. Reminiscent of some of the statements made earlier by Secretary Dulles, Kennedy Administration spokesmen, and General de Gaulle, Brandt's statement called for expanding the relationship between the two parts of Germany. As for "two Germanies," he declared:

> . . . negotiations at Government level without discrimination on either side . . . should lead to contractually agreed cooperation. International recognition of the GDR by the Federal Republic is out of the question. Even if there are two states in Germany, they are not foreign countries to each other; their relations with each other can only be of a special nature.[16]

Parenthetically, Brandt's formulation of the two-state declaration was repeated in his State of the Nation speech of mid-January 1970, in which he spoke of "two states within one German nation." From these two declarations, it can be argued that despite any legal ambiguities, his statements, coupled with pledges to respect the territorial integrity of the GDR—meaning its eastern border on the Oder-Neisse—amount to de facto recognition that two Germanies exist, at least as "an enforced reality."

The Prague Agenda

Given the opportunity to negotiate force renunciations and trade credits, the Eastern states acted within two days of Brandt's October 1969 speech. They met, ironically, in Prague and proposed two items in an open-ended agenda for the proposed East-West European security conference:

1. The ensuring of European security and renunciation of the use of force or threat of its use in the mutual relations among states in Europe.

2. Expansion of trade, economic, scientific and technical relations on the principle of equal rights [read: recognition of the GDR] aimed at the development of political cooperation among European states. [See Appendix C.]

This appeal from Prague on October 31, 1969, called for "The strengthening of peace in Europe . . . as it has been constituted and exists today," meaning a divided Europe and two Germanies. Preparatory work among interested states would include discussion of "other suggestions" for the advancement of "mutually beneficial cooperation among the European states."

As the Brandt government moved toward bilateral exploratory talks with Russia and Poland, a summit meeting of the Pact members took place in early December 1969. The communique from that meeting in Moscow took the form of reassurances to Ulbricht that "equal relations" between the two Germanies required legal recognition of the GDR—heretofore the precondition for talks. However, the thesis that Brandt's two policy statements would be accepted as de facto recognition was apparently confirmed by the rapid initiation of Soviet-West German contacts on a bilateral nonagression pact, and similar discussions have been explored in Polish-West German notes and in the exchange of press releases between Bonn and Pankow.

Meanwhile, in the United States there were new developments affecting American policy on European security. The Mansfield Resolution for reduction of American forces in Europe was reintroduced in the United States Senate on December 1, 1969.[17] (The identical resolution had been introduced early in 1967. On August 20, 1968, the day of the Russian invasion of Czechoslovakia, the press was reporting that Senator Mansfield, then in Europe, had concluded that NATO had outlived its usefulness because the Soviets were likely to employ military force.)

The number of Senators who called for "substantial reductions" of American troop strength grew during 1969 as President Nixon spoke of the need to fight inflation in the economy and pollution in the environment. Despite growing debate over the Mansfield proposal and references to "Europeanizing" European defense, American officials pledged to maintain current force levels in Europe through mid-1971. Administration leaders voiced apprehension over the implications if American forces in Europe were immediately reduced, in view of the "unravelling" effect which such a move would likely have in NATO, and because of possible effects on strategic arms limitation talks (SALT) and German negotiations.

The Western Response

The official American reply to the Soviet proposal to convene a European security conference came in a speech by Secretary Rogers in Brussels on December 6, 1969, at the time of the NATO Ministerial Meeting. He asserted that the agenda suggested by the Warsaw Pact at Prague was "nebulous and imprecise." He added:

> . . . we must be careful not to confuse the process of negotiation with
> elves into a
> o not deal
> properly be
> t countries
> : East-West
> een a basic
> irs, so that
> o meaning;
> ich regular
>
> premature
> possible a
>
> erms of three
>
> ward German

ERRATA

Page 34

Penultimate paragraph, last line: insert "not" before "likely."

......, .. demonstration of Soviet willingness toward improving the situation in and around Berlin," for which Britain, France, the United States, and the Soviet Union have *quadrilateral* responsibility; and

Third, "A positive Warsaw Pact response to our repeated proposals for mutual and balanced force reductions," a *multilateral* undertaking. Mr. Rogers concluded by stating:

> We should favor a negotiation that holds out realistic hope for a reduction of tensions in Europe. But we will not participate in a conference which has the effect of ratifying or acquiescing in the Brezhnev Doctrine.

In their December meeting in Brussels, the NATO Foreign Ministers took a similarly reserved position toward the Soviet proposal and articulated their view in a declaration which was attached to the final communique of their deliberations. (See Appendix B.) The NATO Declaration drew on the principles of deterrence and detente adopted in 1967 by the Harmel report on the future tasks of the Alliance. And it registered again the basic cleavage between the Western view of sovereign equality and nonintervention in internal affairs, on the one hand, and the Soviet concepts of "limited sovereignty" and "preservation of the gains of socialism," on the other. The declaration repeated NATO's formal offer, made at Reykjavik in June 1968, for mutual and balanced force reductions and noted that there had been no response to this proposal for reducing tensions in Europe.

The Federal Republic's *Ostpolitik*, including West Germany's willingness to enter into bilateral agreements on the non-use of force or the threat of force, was endorsed by the NATO Ministers, and once again the West called for economic, technical, and cultural exchanges as part of what should be the "freer movement of people, ideas and information between the countries of East and West." This invitation to the East was broadened to include a suggestion for cooperation in the field of "human environment." Added to these provisions of Western policy was a section, "Perspectives for Negotiation," in which the NATO Ministers encouraged the continuation and intensification of "contacts, discussions or negotiations through all appropriate channels, bilateral or multilateral, believing that progress [toward solution of the concrete issues concerning European security] is most likely to be achieved by discussing in each instance the means most suitable for the subject."

As for the Soviet proposal and the possibility of holding an early conference on European security, the Ministers agreed that "careful advance preparations and prospects of concrete results would in any case be essential." In a muted reference to the caution articulated by Secretary Rogers, the North Atlantic Council stated that progress in the bilateral and multilateral discussions toward resolving the "fundamental questions" would make a major contribution to improving the political atmosphere in Europe. In summary, it is clear from the NATO Declaration that Western diplomacy would not endorse the Eastern conference proposal if that meant ratifying the present division of Europe rather than reducing tensions as part of realistic agreement by the East on approaches to the problems of Berlin, inter-German relations, and mutual force reductions.

In the face of this attitude by the United States and in view of general, though by no means unanimous, support in NATO, the Soviet Union opened the 1970 season by an unusual announcement in an unusual press conference by Foreign Ministry spokesman Leonid Zamyatin.[19] For the first time it became official that the Soviets anticipated American and Canadian participation from the outset of the conference, thus in effect dropping the all-European emphasis. (This had been widely mentioned in numerous "authorized discussions" by East European leaders and informally by the

Russians but had not been made public previously.) Secondly, the reference to convening the conference in the first half of 1970—a special note of urgency which first appeared at Budapest—was changed to the latter half of the year.

Reports from Moscow and from Eastern Europe also revealed an unpublicized Party meeting in Moscow in mid-January at which there was strong opposition to Russian attempts to control preparations for the conference and at which there were efforts by the East Europeans to obtain a modification of the Brezhnev Doctrine.[20] Partly because of this internal disarray and partly because of the lack of support by Western governments, there are now increasing references to a peoples' congress as an alternative to a conference of government representatives and as the next stage of development. In the spring of 1970 it is unclear which way the questions of modalities and timing will turn. But it is safe to assume that the drive for an East-West European security conference will be raised again whenever the Soviets find the timing and balance of advantage suitable.

4   The Main Issues

As the foregoing review of postwar history shows, divided Germany and divided Berlin are literally, as well as figuratively, at the root of the European security problem. Yet they are intermeshed not only with the problem of reducing the military forces which have been deployed on their account but also with the broader security questions and overall climate of East-West relations. Whether or not any of these substantive issues are likely to or should appear on the agenda of one or more security conferences, each of them must be explored in its own right for an understanding of the detente diplomacy and the defense debates of the 1970's.

Germany

One must start, therefore, with the so-called German problem as the sine qua non of any comprehensive approach to European security. The subject of postwar Germany had been raised in 1943 at Teheran, where there was a tentative, if casual, consensus among Roosevelt, Churchill, and Stalin that Germany would have to be dismembered after the war in order to ensure against her ever becoming a threat to peace.[1] But immediate preoccupations at Yalta with the war itself and preparations for the Normandy invasion left little time for analysis of the postwar problems of Western Europe; the dismemberment idea was merely referred for study and eventually dropped. The public's association of Yalta with big-power hegemony, which was reinforced by de Gaulle's complaints about his exclusion from that conference, is erroneous. The so-called spheres of influence arrangement grew out of a Churchill session with Stalin, at a Moscow meeting from which Roosevelt was absent.

The dominant assumption of the wartime Big Three (although whether Stalin ever really shared it is open to question) was that their wartime solidarity would continue by habit, logic, and necessity into the postwar period.

In one prophetic passage of a long letter to Stalin in April 1945, Churchill wrote:

> There is not much comfort in looking into a future where you and the countries you dominate plus the Communist parties of many other states are drawn up on one side, and those who rally to the English-speaking nations and their associates and dominions are on the other. It is quite obvious that their quarrel would tear the world to pieces. All of us leading men on either side who had anything to do with that would be shamed before history.

But even Churchill closed on the note that "I hope there is no word or phrase in this outpouring of my heart which unwittingly gives offense."[2]

Had the accuracy of Churchill's look at the future been realized, and had Britain and the United States been represented at Potsdam by the same leaders who had been coping with Stalin throughout the war, then it is at least conceivable that Russian actions to establish tight control in Poland and elsewhere in Eastern Europe might have been better contained.

The Origins of Discord

For better or worse, the governments, working through the European Advisory Commission—of which the Russians were members—developed the concept of administering occupied Germany as a *single economic unit*, on a four-power basis, with delineated zones of occupation and joint occupation of Berlin. France was given the status of an occupying power largely at American insistence; and her zones in Berlin and Germany were carved out from those of Britain and the United States, since the Russians declined to revise theirs. It was pursuant to these 1944 agreements that British and American forces withdrew from their points of farthest advance—in some cases to a depth of one hundred and fifty miles along a four hundred mile front—rather than pressing on to Berlin.

So strong were the governing assumptions about the essentiality of postwar cooperation with Russia that the West abided by its undertakings even as the Russians were violating theirs. Protests were made, but a showdown was avoided by Western forbearance. The record shows that every reasonable effort was undertaken to give the Russians no grounds for perceiving a threat to their vital interests.

Meanwhile, of course, the two blueprints that were developing separately in the Western and Eastern zones of Germany were divergent in everything from currency reform to reparations to economic rehabilitation—not to mention the basic issue of political orientation. The West had only gradually come to understand that the term "democratic" meant one thing to the English and French and quite another to the Russians, for whom it became a euphemism for "Communist controlled."[3]

The theoretical four-power nature of supervision meant, of course, that Russia had a veto on all-German matters, which enabled her to frustrate the economic imperatives of providing a link between the resources of the Western zones and neighboring Western Europe. Inevitably, the West found it necessary to take a leaf from the Russian behavior in their own zones and to act independently, although the Western motives were short-range economic objectives and an obvious concern with establishing a free economic and political framework for Germany's development. As Secretary of State Marshall said in his report on the Fifth Session of the Council of Foreign Ministers:

> I anticipated great difficulty in reaching a comprehensive agreement, but I did have a hope that we might take three or four fundamental decisions which would permit immediate action by the Four Powers to alleviate the situation in Germany this winter and greatly improve the prospects for all of Europe. That we failed to reach any such agreements is the greatest disappointment.[4]

The Soviet response was to berate the West for violating the Yalta and Potsdam principles of four-power administration, which the Russians themselves had consistently ignored.

The other events of 1947 and 1948—the Marshall Plan, the Truman Doctrine, the Cominform, the coup in Czechoslovakia, and the Brussels Treaty—were the precursors of NATO and are too well known to require detailed review here. These events culminated in the Russian blockade of Berlin in June 1948, which forced the West to maintain a massive military airlift for almost a year to sustain the city. The Soviet blockade was finally ended on a quid pro quo basis for the resumption by the West of interzonal trade.

Negotiations among the wartime allies on peace treaties with Italy, Bulgaria, Hungary, Rumania, and Finland proved frustrating and time consuming, lasting from mid-1945 until early 1947. But agreement on Germany and Austria proved impossible.[5] The deadlock at Moscow was in fact confirmed in London in November 1947, and despite the numerous subsequent attempts chronicled earlier, the German problem has remained on dead center ever since.

Soviet Objectives

In retrospect, it appears quite clear that Soviet objectives for Germany, from the time that the Nazi defeat was first assured, were as follows:

First, and with overriding priority, to ensure that the Eastern Zone, now the German Democratic Republic (GDR), remained firmly in Communist hands; that those hands were responsive to Russian control; and that the industrial power of East Germany was permanently integrated into the Eastern bloc, first by way of reparations, and then through the COMECOM (Council of Mutual Economic Assistance) system.

Second, to seek the westward extension of Communist influence—and with it, Soviet control—to the remainder of Germany.

Third, to weaken the overall power of Western Europe and deny it access to West German economic potential.

Fourth, to prevent West German rearmament.

Although this last objective was understandable, given traditional Russian fears of Germany, the first steps in the direction of German rearmament were not taken by the West. In May 1950, a month before the attack in Korea that would give rise later to American deployments to Europe and a German military contribution to NATO, the United States futilely protested the creation in East Germany of a fifty thousand man "police" force which was trained and equipped as a ground combat army.[6] Nevertheless, the campaign against West German rearmament and membership in NATO was the subject of a Soviet propaganda campaign that has rarely been rivaled; and as noted previously, it gave rise to a number of diplomatic initiatives as well.

That the first objective of Soviet policy toward Germany, namely control of East Germany, had priority is shown by frequent conflicts with the remaining three aims. At times the Soviets have made propaganda plays for German sympathy, and they have even proposed an all-German government, to which the Russians were usually opposed These efforts appear to have been defensive moves; or perhaps they were offensive ventures taken on the few occasions when Soviet political intelligence gave less pessimistic reports on the prospects for Communist control of such a regime. But the Soviets' actions in Berlin and East Germany and their refusal even to communicate with, let alone allow access by, the United Nations Commission to Investigate Conditions for Free Elections in Germany[7] have undercut whatever prospects for success there might have been in the last three objectives.

It should not be necessary to detail here the developments of the late 1940's and early 1950's—the arguments over reparations, the creation in the West of "bizonia" from the British and American zones, then the merging into "trizonia" with the French Zone, and finally, the establishment of the Federal Republic of Germany (FRG) in 1949, the termination of Western occupation in 1952, and West Germany's admission to NATO in 1955.[8] The parallel countersteps by the East involved creation of the East German Democratic Republic in 1949, recognition of it as "sovereign" by the U.S.S.R., and formation of the Warsaw Pact in 1955. The so-called spirit of Geneva, stemming from the summit conference held there in the summer of 1955, failed to thaw the ice that had now frozen the positions in Germany; so the action shifted to Berlin, which had been relatively quiescent since the end of the blockade.

Western Objectives

On the Western side, foreign policy objectives and priorities were also sorting themselves out in the postwar decade; and, as in the East, they centered on Germany. Having rejected the dismemberment proposal of Teheran, and the pastoral-economy concept of the Morgenthau Plan for Germany, the West had to accept the economic realities of Germany's role in Europe. Russian political hostility also forced the Western allies to face political realities which were obscured by the assumptions about the workability of four-power control of Germany as a unit. Moreover, initial Western priorities had been devoted to the pragmatic task of feeding Europe instead of to the longest-range political context.

West Europeans, including many West Germans, were no more anxious than their neighbors to the East to see the Federal Republic rearmed; yet the newborn NATO faced not only a verbal threat but also a better than five-to-one military superiority in Europe. Although NATO was supplemented by an American atomic deterrent, it could be accurately described as "minimum" until well after the Korean War. Germany was the only source for redressing, even in part, the military imbalance without impeding Western Europe's economic recovery. This posed great problems for the French, who, according to a witticism of the day, wanted a German army larger than the Russians' but smaller than their own.

The solution was to extend the integration formula initiated by the Schuman Plan, already underway in the economic field and being considered in the political area as a way of burying what Churchill called the "hatreds and revenges which have sprung from the injuries of the past." When France failed to ratify the proposed European Defense Community (EDC), Western statesmen revived the Western European Union (WEU) and remodeled it into a vehicle for containing West German rearmament and tying those forces to NATO.[9]

Even in the Federal Republic, where there were considerable pressures to avoid German integration in the West (at the presumed cost of abandoning hope for reunification), the priorities under Chancellor Adenauer were generally in line with those of the West as a whole. Thus, first priority was the meshing of a democratic Germany into the political and economic life of the West; second, to maintain the legal status quo while seeking the reunification of Germany on the basis of free elections. As in the East, there was an inherent conflict between policies toward the parts of Germany and policies toward the whole. A freely elected all-German government would presumably not be Communist; yet no Western power could really have faced the prospect of a united Germany allied with Russia, with Communist power thereby extended through the heart of Europe to the Rhine. And if there were no such prospect, could the Russians run the contrary risk of having NATO at the borders of Poland?

The Incompatible Preferences

Lining up the two sets of priorities for the East and West, as sketched above, it is easy to see why they are incompatible:

	East	West
Most Preferred	Germany unified, Communist, and allied to the Eastern Bloc	Germany unified and allied to West
Preferred	East Germany tied to Bloc; West Germany "neutral"	West Germany integrated with West Europe; East Germany "neutral"
Status quo	East Germany tied to Bloc; West Germany allied to West	West Germany allied to West; East Germany tied to Bloc
Least Preferred	Germany unified and truly neutral	Germany unified and truly neutral
Unacceptable	Germany unified and allied to West	Germany unified and allied to East

Hypothetical room for agreement or change in the status quo can be found only in the least preferred case. The West's most preferred arrangement is the East's unacceptable, and vice versa; and so on, down the preference ladder.

Accordingly, the status quo may well seem preferable to the lowest category of theoretical acceptability. If the earlier supposition is correct, namely that the top Soviet priority is to avoid the loss of East Germany, then no change in the status quo is possible, unless the economic strain of the arms race, the desire for West German disarmament, or concern with China leads to a restructuring of Soviet priorities. In fact, in the absence of such restructuring, the West would do well to look suspiciously at any Russian willingness to seek a "neutral" unified Germany— since it logically would have to be based upon a Soviet belief that a later Communist take-over from within was possible or that Russia could outbid the West for the allegiance of a "neutral" Germany. Such a "Rapallo of the 1970's" would not bode well for the stability of Europe or of the world. On the other hand, Russia, not without reason, has been suspicious of Western advocacy of German unification because of the greater economic and political magnetism which the West would undoubtedly exert.

The goal of German reunification in Western foreign policies has had a strange and somewhat ironic history.[10] Growing out of pragmatic postwar-occupation concerns, it became ensconced as a goal by virtue of being the best basis for demonstrating Russian intransigence and because of its political appeal within West Germany. Yet the phenomenal growth of German economic strength (and, although somewhat latent in comparison, Germany's development of political power) makes it problematic now whether Germany's neighbors any longer seriously desire this declaratory goal of the 1950's. And some, no doubt, would have a clear preference for maintaining a permanent separation of West Germany's sixty million residents and one hundred and forty billion dollar gross national product from East Germany's twenty million people and thirty billion dollar gross national product.

In Germany itself, religious, economic, and social factors in the GDR, plus the fact that the many refugees who left the East are now fairly well settled, may make reunification less desired in fact than is articulated politically. Chancellor Brandt seems to be proceeding on this assumption; but this does not necessarily reduce the danger of backlash in West German politics.

In the short term, an "Austrian neutrality" solution for Germany is therefore a dubious prospect at best. Germany would simply be too large a politico-military-economic entity—and therefore quite unlike Austria or Sweden—to be allowed to wander from East to West in search of its destiny and possibly acquire a new nationalism in the process.

It is hard to reach any conclusion other than that there are no available solutions in the short term for the problem of Germany, other than minor variants on a status quo which neither side is willing or able to change by force. From the Western point of view, however, there are some important variants to be considered, for example on Berlin, before entering any de jure formalization of the de facto status quo. Another consideration has to be the long-term future of the German "nation", which, given the impasse described above, must be perceived in the context of a wider reconciliation between the two halves of Europe, if not, indeed, of the world. That is why some statesmen, for example Willy Brandt,[11] and some scholars, for example Zbigniew Brzezinski[12], speak of a "prolonged process" and the importance of "movement" for its own sake. Yet it would be unwise to have too much hope, for the processes of change move slowly, and the risks of true detente to the Soviet and Eastern European regimes appear to be well above the post-Czechoslovakia tolerance level of the Soviet system.

But this is not to say that some form of confederal arrangement, if not federal relations—probably within clearly described limits—cannot develop between the two Germanies without setting in motion the fears on which the conflicting perference scales are based. This would permit the settling of such matters as Germany's boundaries, which are now relatively noncontroversial, and permit some quiet amelioration of the lot of the East Germans—a goal on which the Federal Republic can quite rightly insist.

This appears to be Brandt's objective in his exploratory talks with East Germany, which have the backing of his major allies. But almost of necessity, this must proceed from a kernel of agreement arrived at through quiet diplomacy. It is hard to see a role for a European security conference in this connection, except as the product of a process aimed at formal ratification of a whole series of new understandings, German-German, East-West, West-West, and East-East, which have not even started to emerge. In the meantime, the role of a conference would appear to be purely theatrical as far as German reunification is concerned—except for the prospect, on which Ulbricht counts, that increased "recognition" and international status for East Germany would flow from mere attendance at such a conference.

Berlin

Berlin is part and parcel of the overall German problem, as well as an issue in itself. Paradoxically, there may be a better framework for approaching its problems through four-power diplomacy than as part of the German question as a whole, for Berlin retains the international juridical status acquired in 1945 as occupied territory administered by the Four Powers. As we have seen, the four-power rubric has almost entirely disappeared (although the military liaison missions established at Potsdam do continue to function) in both East and West Germany. It is retained, however in Berlin, faute de mieux. In theory the Russians still recognize quadripartite status of the city, despite previous threats to turn over their responsibilities to Pankow (the Berlin suburb where the East German government set up its capitol); but in practice, Moscow applies this status only to West Berlin.[13]

Presumably, the Russians and East Germans still consider West Berlin—as in Khrushchev's metaphoric description to Kennedy—to be a "bone in their throat," to be removed sooner or later. The construction of the Berlin Wall to stanch the hemorrhage of refugees from East to West has now brought some stability and anesthesized the pain to the GDR. But the Eastern objective of eliminating West Berlin's special legal status remains. The 1948-1949 Russian blockade was one attempt to achieve that goal; the "Thanksgiving" ultimatum (November 27, 1958) was another; and the last was the June 1961 threat to sign a separate peace treaty with the German Democratic Republic. In the twenty-year war of nerves, the West consistently refused to be driven or threatened out of Berlin; and it has insisted on treating with the East Germans, if at all, only as agents of the Russians, whose legal responsibility could not be abrogated unilaterally. Substantial force buildups have been generated on both sides by the major Berlin crises; and in the end, the Soviet Union did not press its claim to the point of war. Usually the cycle of tensions has alternated with cycles of "summitry"—meetings at the heads-of-government level, as in Geneva in 1955, Camp David in 1959, the abortive Paris Summit of 1960, and the Glassboro meeting of July 1967.

But quite apart from the cycle of big crises and major diplomatic initiatives, the little crises over Western access have continued. One of these, which involved the deliberate delay of an American military convoy, occurred at the precise moment the Secretary of State and the Russian Ambassador were signing a major agreement on wheat deliveries to the Soviet Union, a trade measure hailed as a symbol of new understanding. One can only speculate whether this was deliberate or coincidental—as with the American bombing of Hanoi while Kosygin was visting there. The reader need not be burdened with the story of "games" people have played over Berlin, it should suffice to say that these have ranged from aircraft harassment to arguments over flags on military trains and whether tailgates of military trucks in convoys should be up or down and the soldiers dismounted for counting. The Soviet objective has been, of course, to tighten the degree of Russian de facto control and, if possible, to give East Germany the "sovereign" regulation of Western access. The legal rights for Western military access are both implicit, in the Potsdam accords, and explicit, in numerous four-power documents of the immediate postwar period.[14]

West German civilian access, the city's critical lifeblood, has for the most part depended in practice on the quid pro quo of interzonal trade agreements; although in extremis, as the airlift showed, it too may depend on allied military access. The problem has been quiescent, in comparative terms at least, for a considerable period. But by accident or design, it could become again a flash point of renewed tension. The Berlin corn on the West's toe can, to use another colorful Khrushchevism, be stepped on at will.

In summary, the West has been successful in maintaining the besieged bastion of West Berlin and the critical access thereto during more than twenty years of recurrent challenge. But the Western three have retained only a nominal quadripartite hand in East Berlin. For its part, the East has been successful in obtaining de facto if not de jure annexation of East Berlin and posing the "problem" purely in terms of resolving the "abnormality" in the Western part of the city. Khrushchev spoke to Kennedy about the possibility of *West* Berlin's becoming a "free city," but he never replied to—nor have his successors—the obvious riposte that all of Berlin must be included in any settlement. On this point, the Russian and East German leadership have so far swallowed their own propaganda directed against West German political activities in West Berlin, and they complain at the slightest evidence of any Western action that might violate the postwar Potsdam and four-power decrees. Meanwhile, Ulbricht and the Soviets openly permit East German military parades and overflights of the entire city, and they proclaim East Berlin to be the capital of East Germany. Propaganda aside, however, Russia has never quite burned the bridge to a quadripartite basis for negotiations.

Realistically speaking, it is hard to see what other outcome to the Berlin stalemate was possible, for West Berlin remains militarily untenable, an island in a hostile sea, at least one hundred miles from a safe "shore." Only Western political and economic commitments—the most solemn assurances to the people of West Berlin by five American Presidents, statements by scores of Western Prime Ministers and in numerous NATO ministerial meetings, plus billions of dollars invested in the economic viability and growth of the city—have made credible to the Russians an otherwise incredible proposition: that the West would risk nuclear war, if necessary, to preserve the Berlin status quo against forcible change. But deterrence could not be effective in East Berlin where these factors—plus even a minimal permanent Western military presence—were missing. For essentially the same reasons, there was little that the West could have done about the Wall. In fact, an argument can be made that by stopping the hemorrhage, the East saved itself from a disaster of such magnitude that the only way out might have been to seize West Berlin and run the real risk of nuclear war.

Despite relative quiet in recent years, the situation cannot be called a healthy one. Access is vulnerable to constant harassments; one was in process concurrently with Ulbricht's initially favorable response to Bonn's overtures for talks.[15] The growing desire to give West Berlin as much participation in West German political life as is consistent with the "occupation" nature of the West's legal position there is increasingly subject to East German challenge, with fluctuating degrees of Russian encouragement.[16]

Moreover, as younger generations emerge, the degree of interest in support for the West's position in Berlin may ebb. Yet, in Berlin, as in Germany as a whole, agreed changes to the status quo are hard to visualize. The West became too committed during the years of challenge to find a face-saving way to withdraw; to leave now, it could be argued, would threaten the credibility of too many other commitments, many of which are comparatively much less formal and solemn. And the East is now similarly committed to the status of East Berlin. The politicians of both East and West Germany would be unlikely to survive a dramatic change of the status quo in Berlin in either direction. Nor would Russia or the West force a solution, at this cost.

All parties concerned might, in theory at least, be able to agree on a phase-out, over several years, of the West's position in West Berlin in exchange for a suitable quid pro quo. But it is hard to imagine one of sufficient value to compensate for the enormous investments already made in West Berlin; and the West Berliners wishing to leave would need a chance to relocate under favorable economic conditions. If East Germany were to give up, say, the entire region of Thuringia, which bulges into West Germany (an area of some three to four thousand square miles) and share in the costs of relocating people, an "exchange of territory" might be remotely possible. But the complexities of such a deal stagger the imagination.

Possible Solutions

An all-Berlin solution, if one were possible, would escape some of the unrealities and dangers of the all-German solution that were outlined above; as a pilot project in European security, it might prove to be a way station to German reunification. For example, a neutral and reunified "free city" would allow the West to say that they have regained the East, and permit the East to argue the reverse within its constituency. To be sure, the East would still fear the "infection potential" of a free city and economy; but the newly reunited city would not contain the Western military and intelligence operations about which the East constantly complains. In the Berlin question, the zero-sum game or your-gain-is-my-loss characteristics of the overall German problem are somewhat less; and the risks of the least-preferred genuine-neutrality solution are also less significant to both sides. For unlike Germany as a whole, Berlin is not too large an entity for an "Austrian" approach.

The West would have to consider what guarantees could be obtained for the continued viability—against access interference and internal subversion—of such an all-Berlin solution. Mere pledges would hardly suffice, given the years of broken promises already experienced. Making Berlin a major international city, perhaps under the United Nations, with the active presence of international agencies and staffs, might give some assurance. This might include the foundation of an East-West European Institute for the study of environmental and ecological problems. In addition, formally specified road, rail, and air links, almost an international corridor in which Russian and East German controls would be inoperative, might be needed. Failing this, Western access rights might have to be retained. Without such assurances of viability, however, the all-Berlin solution of internationalization would seem a risky proposition at best.

Thus, one can conceive, in theory at least, of a Berlin settlement within the known parameters—an arrangement which does not depend on a prior solution to the German question. But the East has shown little signs of interest in this possibility, except as it might apply exclusively to West Berlin. This is the old familiar approach of "What is ours is ours and what is yours is negotiable" that makes dealing with the Communists so frustrating. But a European security conference hardly seems a likely setting for the delicate compromise, and perhaps trade and financial inducements, which any such agreement would entail.

One also needs to consider the possibility of approaching the Berlin problem within the larger German context, perhaps in such a way as to facilitate at least an interim arrangement to the latter. As explained above, making Berlin the unified capital of a unified and neutral Germany appears out of the question at present; but there is another possibility, albeit a radical and perhaps impractical one, to which there have been references in German literature.[17] It also comes up from time to time when Western governments start to review their homework. This idea proposes the creation of an artificial new state of Middle Germany—in effect a buffer zone made up of territory ceded by both East and West Germany along the present demarcation line, including all of Berlin. (A variant, even more radical in some ways, would be to divide East Germany on a diagonal line through Berlin, with the northeast part going to Poland, and the southwest to West Germany. This might please the Poles, perhaps the Federal Republic, and conceivably even the Russians. But it is hard to imagine any enthusiasm on the part of the East Germans who would become Polish, and especially on the part of Herr Ulbricht.)

A look at a map shows how unnatural a state Middle Germany would be: a narrow strip, fifty to eighty miles wide, stretching some five hundred miles along the eastern frontier of the Federal Republic from Austria to the Baltic, having a triangular shape in the middle, and cutting over one hundred miles into East Germany to encompass Berlin. The lines could be gerrymandered to leave a viable East Germany, with such major industrial centers as Dresden and Leipzig untouched, and to avoid major West German cities such as Nuremberg, Hannover, and Hamburg. All three Germanies—West, Middle, and

East—might then form a confederation for all-German internal and economic affairs, leaving the political system and alliances of East and West untouched. Such a confederation, however, could negotiate and ratify its external boundaries as part of a wider settlement. (The reader who calls this, not unification, but triplication is reminded that this is precisely what was required [i.e., establishing the United States Air Force] in order to unify the U. S. Department of Defense in 1947, where feelings for and against unification were strongly held by the Army and Navy, respectively.)

The problem, of course, would be that such an artificial creation would hardly be viable without a high degree of East-West cooperation. Also, this buffer state might prove vulnerable to pressures from the East. The politics of Middle Germany would be especially difficult. But perhaps a variant of the Austrian or Finnish model would be acceptable to both sides; and the real advantage might be a truly disarmed and neutral zone in the center of Europe, an idea that has been central to many European security proposals. Starting with this international agreement, the next decade might well see such genuine progress toward European security as gradual disengagement and troop withdrawals from the present line of confrontation. In the meantime, the risk of incidents or accidental superpower conflict which could escalate would be dramatically lowered. Even more than the all-Berlin solution, however, such a radical approach would require a consensus on far broader issues, to which the previous comments on Germany and the security conference apply.

There is a final possibility—one to which the East now objects violently but which it might conceivably come to accept as part of a package arrangement between East and West Germany in exchange for a Western agreement ending adherence to the occupation rubric and "recognizing" the present incorporation of East Berlin into the GDR. This possibility would be a treaty signed by all powers concerned and according West Berlin the constitutional status of a *Land* (State) in the Federal Republic, a city-state enclave that would be protected by West Germany and NATO just like any other part of the treaty area, although possibly subject to a ceiling on troop levels in West Berlin. Even if a new agreement spelled out formal access rights to be guaranteed by all parties, this would still not insure against trouble; but as an exercise in de facto ratification of the status quo, this arrangement could be a small step toward an interim solution similar to internationalization or the establishment of a buffer zone Middle Germany. And as in the latter cases, superpower agreement on this major European security issue would decrease considerably the risks of clashes between the troops of the adversaries who directly face each other at the Berlin Wall.

To recapitulate, the order of Eastern preferences for "solving" the Berlin issue appears to be (1) elimination of the West's position in Berlin and extension of full Communist control to the entire city; (2) elimination of the Western allies' rights and of Bonn's claims in West Berlin and transformation of that part of the city into a special international entity. Both of these preferences are unacceptable to the West, which could conceivably, however, accept either version of an all-Berlin solution (as the capital of Middle Germany or as a special international city with guaranteed access) or the West Berlin-merger-with-West Germany alternative under suitable guarantees. Which of these two Western-preferred outcomes would be least unacceptable to the East cannot be predicted with certainty. But it can readily be seen that the hypothetical margin for agreement is small, if indeed it exists at all.

In the absence of a more definitive solution, the status quo in Berlin must continue, even though it is satisfactory to neither side. There are, however, other ways of making the existing situation more tolerable both in German relationships and among the Four Powers. Steps to explore both of these dimensions appear to be in progress. As part of his overall *Ostpolitik,* Chancellor Brandt has agreed to meet East German Premier Stoph in East Berlin, where he may well seek to counter demands for full legal recognition of East Germany by proposing discussions of such practical measures as renewal of the visitor-pass arrangements; coordination of telecommunications, transport, postal service, and the like; as well as the improvement of economic relations between the "two states in the German nation" and between the two parts of Berlin. The Russians have replied affirmatively to the Western request for four-power talks on Berlin, although they imply that they want to discuss only West Berlin.[18]

The West, therefore, may have to make it clear that the Russians can have it one way or the other; that is, either the quadripartite agreements of 1945 still apply to all of Berlin or, alternatively, one can consider substituting new arrangements for the entire city. But the Soviet Union cannot logically or legally have it both ways: unilateral abrogation in East Berlin and a quadripartite role in the West. Such plain talk by Western diplomats could risk a setback to detente hopes, but it also might clear the air sufficiently for some useful understandings, even informal ones, on West German activities in West Berlin and access matters, so as to defuse the most dangerous aspects of the Berlin problem. Any further amelioration, however, would have to depend upon the progress in improving relations between the two Germanies.

Mutual Force Reductions

Mutual force reductions are not yet agreed upon as an issue of European security, for the Warsaw Pact has not replied to NATO's invitations to discuss the matter. One reason for this is that the Soviet Union can expect to overcome whatever pressures may exist for reduction or redeployment of forces in Eastern Europe; and they must have confidence that the pressures represented by the Mansfield and Symington resolutions in the U.S. Senate will eventually achieve a unilateral Western, or at least American, reduction with no concessions required on their part. Moreover, even if they believed that such Western reductions would allow them, militarily speaking, to follow suit, there would be political arguments against emulation.

The Pact's Problem

Soviet forces in Germany, Poland, Hungary, and now Czechoslovakia, serve a dual purpose: first, they have a normal defense—and deterrence—function and back up Eastern diplomacy vis-à-vis the West in general and West Germany in particular; second, they maintain internal security and assure not only the continued power of local Communist parties but also, as in Czechoslovakia, their fidelity to Moscow.

Parenthetically, although the Russians boast of having no military-industrial complex,[19] it is at least a fair question whether the many senior billets and other perquisites which go with the maintenance of several army groups in Eastern Europe do not exert a subtle effect on structure and policy. Certainly, honesty requires an admission that there is a degree of such influence in Western military politics.

Russia has bilateral security pacts with each Warsaw Pact member—a network of treaties which would support the military status quo should the pact itself ever have to be jettisoned—for example in connection with the familiar dissolution-of-pacts propaganda line.[20] (As a matter of interest, NATO's detailed status-of-forces agreements are basically multilateral, with the rights and obligations of "sending" and "receiving" states spelled out in the London and the Ottawa agreements which supplement the NATO Treaty itself. There are no American bilateral security treaties with the individual European members of NATO except those agreements which cover nuclear weapons stockpiles. This is why French withdrawal from the military side of NATO presented an unprecedented problem insofar as French forces in West Germany were concerned. In bilateral conversations, France and the Federal Republic finally agreed to leave them there by mutual consent.)

That is not to say that Soviet force levels in Eastern Europe are completely insensitive to changes in the threat as they perceive it. A Western reduction should logically call for an even greater reduction on the Soviet side—greater in proportion to the longer distances involved in withdrawing American and Canadian forces if one sought a man-mile equivalency. But the threat involved in the Soviet internal security mission is only marginally one of Western military or even political potential; it is primarily inherent in the changing politics of the socialist bloc and the liberalizing tendencies in Eastern Europe.

With only covert help from the Russians, the Czech Communist Party took that country into the Russian camp in 1948. Twenty years later, the Russians had to put in more than one hundred thousand soldiers to be sure of keeping it there. The Russians appeared to have learned a lesson about crisis management from their experience in Hungary in 1956: when you move in force, do it decisively—and massively. So despite the argument that Soviet deployments are excessive for internal security reasons alone, one must consider the unreliability and possible hostility, from the viewpoint of the Soviet planner, of satellite armed forces. To neutralize them, and present the country being "protected" with a picture of such overwhelming force that resistance is useless could well require at least the present Soviet deployments. The total Warsaw Pact forces used in the Czechoslovakian operation (not all within that country, however) involved three hundred thousand men in twenty-five divisions, plus their combat and logistic support, some of which came from the Baltic and other Russian military districts, as well as a sizable air force.[21]

There are currently thirty-two Soviet divisions in Central and Eastern Europe—twenty in the Group of Soviet Forces in Germany (GSFG), three in Poland, four in Hungary, and five in Czechosolvakia. Given the organization of Russian ground forces, it is hard to envisage any significant room for reduction except in the first category (GSFG) and perhaps eventually in Czechoslovakia. East Germany and Hungary each have six divisions, and the Poles and Czechs each have fourteen, for a total of forty—probably only half of which can be considered combat ready, and all of which suffer from some question of reliability from the Russian point of view.[22]

One could speculate that at least five Soviet and perhaps five satellite divisions (or about fifteen percent of the total) might be deployed or demobilized without degrading the internal security capability below the level which a Soviet planner might regard as acceptable. NATO might well set its initial sights on negotiating on East-West reduction of forces within these parameters.

NATO and the Military Balance

Looking at the matter from NATO's standpoint, the reader may be surprised to learn that there are still widespread disagreements on the existing balance of opposing forces in Europe. One of the best unclassified sources of information about this East-West balance is in the publications of the Institute for Strategic Studies, whose 1969-1970 comparative table is reprinted, with permission, as Appendix A. It shows that NATO has about two-thirds of the manpower, forty percent of the tanks, and half of the tactical aircraft—though about as many fighter/ground attack types—as the Warsaw Pact, in terms of more or less combat-ready forces. In most categories, especially in firepower, the quality of Western units is higher.

Moreover, NATO has more men under arms and spends more money on defense than the Warsaw Pact, and it also has greater civilian manpower and industrial resources. NATO could probably achieve close to parity, if granted sufficient time for mobilization and deployments from the United States and elsewhere. But secrecy, distance, and other mobilization asymmetries make the "M-Day Plus" balance uncertain; and even if the West got the warning time which it anticipates having, probably correctly, then there are questions as to whether NATO would choose to escalate an incipient crisis by using that time to call up reserves and deploy augmentation forces. With respect to active ground forces, a mere count of divisions—more than two to one for the Pact in the Central Region—does not accurately indicate the military balance, since NATO divisions are almost fifty percent larger and have greater staying power.

Nevertheless, some Europeans have been heard to argue that the duration of NATO's ability to defend against a full-scale Soviet attack would be better measured by a clock than a calendar. Yet, on the other hand, some optimists apparently believe that NATO could reduce its force level and still balance the Warsaw Pact.[23]

The calculation of the East-West military balance in Europe is extremely complex, with many unknowns and some unknowables, particularly in the dynamics of combat operations. The analysis is plagued by incommensurables, the "unquantifiable," and manifold uncertainties. How does one analyze the interaction of the air battle with the ground engagement? How valuable are indices of comparative firepower, given entirely different tactics and organization between Western and Eastern armies? What about the intangibles of leadership, morale and luck? The attacker—we always assume it is they, and they doubtless assume it is we—has the considerable advantage of surprise; but conventional military wisdom calls for a numerical superiority of three to one for a successful attack, that is, a much greater ratio of force to space. Most important, the nuclear weapons available to both sides add the major uncertainty. Even if not used, the possibility that a defender might initiate the use of nuclear weapons inhibits an attacker from massing his forces. And so on.

In view of the incommensurables, one might conclude that the extremist on both sides are not only wrong but dangerously wrong. For both sides star from a premise and then select their figures and scenarios to match, arguin, from "best" and "worst" cases, respectively.

Anyone who wants to prove that no money need be spent on conventiona forces since nuclear weapons must be used at the outset of conflict anyway can find or invent figures to support him. But so can anyone who wants to argue that the conventional military balance is close enough so that th dangers of nuclear reliance can be avoided entirely or that American or othe Western forces can be reduced.

But unless deterrence fails, we are not talking about an actual East-Wes military engagement; we are talking, rather, about the political interaction o two sets of perceptions, both of which are colored toward conservatism. Propaganda aside, the Russians probably do have scenarios in which reinforced NATO forces successfully invade Eastern Europe. The laughter o: NATO's Generals at such a proposition would probably be echoed by th Pact's Marshals if they heard some of NATO's inflated estimates of thei: offensive capabilities. The relevant point is that neither side's military expert; can write a scenario with sufficient confidence in a favorable outcome to convince their political superiors to take major risks. If the possibilities for ; fait accompli are blocked, then the prospects for dangerous escalation from ; major military engagement become too significant; and the ultimate step o the escalation ladder is central strategic war, in which victor and vanquishe might be indistinguishable.

A balanced political-military view—and one which appears to be that o NATO's Defense Ministers—is that the present quantitative level of forces i about right to maintain a credible deterrent in Europe and that, in th absence of "mutual force reductions balanced in scope and timing," it must be maintained.* Curiously, both those who attack this judgment as to optimistic and those who claim it is too pessimistic arrive at but on conclusion: NATO can reduce unilaterally. They reach this conclusion by opposite routes, however. The optimist argues that Western military strengt is more than sufficient; the pessimist maintains that NATO forces are too small to be meaningful.

---

*The Ministers have also concluded, however, that those qualitative deficiencies in NATO which can be corrected without sizable increases in defense budgets must be remedied. The recently issued 1970 British White Paper on defense reflects a NATC consensus in saying that the Alliance has just barely "sufficient conventional forces to contain anything but a major deliberate attack," for which nuclear weapons would have to be employed.

These critics are joined by a large and growing group who perceive no military threat at all and therefore believe that the whole argument is irrelevant: "World War II is ancient history; the Russians are preoccupied with their own problems, so just bring the troops home and nothing will happen."

Unfortunately, the world is not so simple. As noted earlier, the issues left by the war with Germany could not be solved, partly because of conflicting Russian and Western interests in the future of Germany. They still conflict. The East is willing to accept the status quo because NATO and the American presence make it too risky to change it in their favor. Remove that risk, and the drive to change it might reappear. The disarray and insecurity which would follow a substantial American troop withdrawal from Western Europe could create temptations for the Kremlin of a very destablizing kind. For totalitarian regimes in trouble at home sometimes seek to unify dissenters or at least to divert their energies by finding distractions abroad.

We need not even postulate a direct military aggression; a Europe which became disproportionately weak vis-à-vis Russia would have little choice but to accommodate, as Finland has done, to the sometimes subtle but always present external pressure, both in its internal politics and foreign policies. Given the extent and definition of American interests in European security, this is unacceptable.

Under Secretary of State Richardson recently presented a careful public exposition of the Nixon Administration's position on West European security and the importance of maintaining American forces through the "era of negotiation."[24] Senator Mansfield promptly replied that Europeans have been "safe and comfortable" in a status quo defended by Americans for twenty years, and the Senator saw no reason why two hundred and fifty million Europeans cannot organize an effective defense against "200 million Russians who are contending at the same time with 700 million Chinese."[25] Unfortunately, there is not one but several reasons.

First, NATO-Europe is not a single entity with taxing and spending powers; it is a grouping of thirteen countries ranging from two hundred thousand to sixty-one million in population—states which are still in the first stages of a long-term unification process. And each country has a different problem: France, thanks to de Gaulle's legacy, has an ambivalent attitude toward NATO; Britain, now more "Europe-oriented," has a chronic balance-of-payments problem; Belgium is beset by linguistic factionalism, and Italy by domestic instability; Germany cannot substantially increase its forces without alarming both allies and enemies; and so on.

Second, even with the small forces of Britain and France, Europe lacks nuclear power on a scale sufficient to cope unaided with that of a thermonuclear superpower. And the nuclear Nonproliferation Treaty, which the United States spent years negotiating as a matter of basic world interest, prohibits the development of additional European nuclear forces and any American nuclear aid, at least until "Europe" becomes a unitary state, which is not a short-run prospect.

Moreover, West Europeans would have to triple their present defense spending—to over twelve percent of gross economic product, which would be one of the world's highest—in order to match the annual defense budget of the Soviet Union, whose disadvantages in having other "fronts" to worry about (especially China) are offset by the advantages of an economy of scale and a central decision-making mechanism.

Western Europe probably could match this level of defense expenditure as a matter of economics; but one can put at close to zero the probability that this could be achieved politically in present circumstances, that is, without bringing to power reactionary leadership of a type which would be destabilizing and dangerous in the long run. Finally, such a Fortress Europe might well trigger genuine concerns in the East of a type which could fatally impede hopes for a gradual reduction of East-West tensions and a long-term security settlement. Significantly, any strategically meaningful European increase would have to come from the Federal Republic, which would certainly seem provocative to the Warsaw Pact and could be profoundly disturbing to Europe as a whole.

A "substantial" American withdrawal, as that term is used by Senate critics,[26] might have similar effects, because it would be believed by the Europeans to be the beginning of the end. Given the precarious military balance that now exists, to seriously erode the high-quality American nucleus—which also controls the nuclear stockpiles in Europe—would be seen as a fatal weakening of the entire security system in Europe.

Burden Sharing in NATO

Senator Mansfield and his colleagues have raised another issue of long-standing concern to Congress, namely, a more equitable sharing of the burden of resources devoted to Western defense. As with questions about the current military balance, one can argue burden sharing equally well from either direction: for example, it is true that the United States, like the Soviet Union, has been spending about nine percent of its gross national product for defense—more than twice the West European average—and spends each year what a larger number of Europeans manage to spend in four. (However, Secretary Laird's projection for fiscal 1971 calls for defense expenditures which amount to only seven percent of American gross national product.)[27]

Alternatively, one can argue that the United States incurs from about one third up to one half of NATO's total annual defense costs, depending on how these costs are calculated[28] —whereas it has nearly two thirds of NATO's total gross national product. Americans seem willing to accept progressive taxation at home—in other words, the principle that the wealthier pay higher rates. But they apparently reject the notion that this principle is equitable internationally, that is, for a country with two and one-half times the average per capita income of the Alliance to pay at least twice as high a defense "tax"—although this is just about the case in some American personal income tax brackets.

On balance, the inequity is not so great as to be an iniquity—unless, of course, European defense is viewed merely as a form of foreign aid quite unrelated to America's own vital interests. On the other hand, West Europeans seem well advised to take account of the very real political sentiments in the United States favoring large-scale troop withdrawals and to make it feasible for the Nixon Administration to continue its policy of holding the line. (At the December 1969 meeting of NATO Defense Ministers, the United States agreed to maintain its present force levels in Europe through the end of fiscal 1971, that is, until June 30, 1971.)[29] And there is some evidence that they are doing so:

—West Europeans took the lion's share, some ninety percent, of the one billion dollar post-Czechoslovakia increase in NATO defense budgets.

—There is a general understanding that West European defense budgets will be increased as much as four percent annually in real terms (amounting to a twenty-percent increase, over and above losses to inflation, during the current five-year planning period) to correct certain qualitative shortcomings in NATO forces. Only Britain (and France) joined the United States in decreasing total defense expenditures in 1969 as against 1968. Italy's stayed the same, and all others increased. Britain's defense spending for 1970-1971, however, is projected to increase to five and one-half percent of the country's gross national product.[30]

—The United States now uses more of NATO's commonly financed infrastructure (airfields, pipelines, and communications) than it pays for—a reversal of the situation a few years ago and another shift in burden sharing.

—The French decision to request NATO's departure from France has led to a fascinating international legal wrangle—collectively with the other fourteen Alliance members and bilaterally with the United States (and Canada to a lesser extent). Substantial claims have been presented under both headings involving investment costs of hundreds of millions of dollars.[31] The other thirteen members of the Alliance have undertaken to reimburse the

United States for the reestablishment outside France of those American facilities which support NATO. These relocation costs are also subject to an American claim against France for requiring the moves, but the risks of French nonpayment for this part of the total claim fall on West European, rather than on American, taxpayers, which is an unprecedented European contribution to burden sharing.

Canada's decision to withdraw from Western Europe some of her small contingent of ground and air forces went in the other direction from the generally encouraging Allied response during the past few years, and some of the smaller European members are not carrying their weight. Britain's energetic Defense Minister Denis Healey has sought to develop a more effective "European caucus" and has promised NATO some of the British forces withdrawn from East of Suez. France may tactily strengthen the coordination between her forces and NATO. The Dutch have started an important and expensive modernization program. And West Germany and Italy have resisted domestic pressures for reductions. In addition to an increase in spending on her own forces, the Federal Republic has generally been helpful in alleviating the balance-of-payments costs of American and British forces stationed on her territory. For 1970-1971, the American-German offset agreement provides for an inflow of one and one-half billion dollars to the United States, sixty percent of which will be for German procurement and forty percent for various financial measures. This sum covers about four fifths of the American payments-imbalance with West Germany. However, there are currently strong complaints from Senator Charles Percy and others about a premature cashing in of certain special American bonds held by the Bundesbank.[32]

The balance-of-payments problem has long been a thorn in the side of America's overseas deployments. A case can be made that annual arm-twisting sessions on a bilateral basis are less effective in the long term than a multilateral-payments scheme under NATO auspices; but the complications —not the least of which is that West Germany has such a large share of the surplus on military account—have so far seemed formidable. The redeployment scheme developed by Secretary McNamara has produced only a portion of the gold-flow savings originally estimated for the thirty-five thousand men who were "dual based"—and of course American troop withdrawals save no money in budgetary costs unless the troops are demobilized. Even then, the budgetary savings would be small in the context of the general phase-down of American general-purpose forces due to Vietnam.

For the long term, if no multilateral framework can be found, the West Germans may have to face the prospect of picking up some of the more onerous support costs (in terms of the bilateral payments-imbalance) for

American forces, such as local labor, utilities, and services, despite the German sensitivity to any form of subsidy which smacks of the "occupation costs" they once had to pay. But the stability of the American military presence is too important to the Federal Republic and to the other European allies not to exhaust all efforts to find a viable solution.

Taking everything into account, one can look at the NATO glass either as half-full or half-empty; and a number of experienced critics believe that the former view is a more accurate, as well as a more useful, perspective.

But suppose Congressional pressures force a large-scale American troop withdrawal? Might this not galvanize the West Europeans into pooling their defense resources and filling the gap? The argument is persuasive that it would not; for the Europeans would believe either that the United States had made some sort of "hegemonial" deal with the Russians in the strategic arms limitation talks (SALT) and foresaw no threat to Europe from that source, which would certainly lead them to decrease their own efforts, or that the United States had devalued its own interest in Europe. Paradoxically, the latter conclusion would probably also lead to the result of reduced European force levels. After all, it is the American military presence which makes it strategically relevant, and hence politically possible, for the small West European countries to sustain and improve their own defenses. Without this validating sine qua non, that is, without a substantial American presence and commitment, West Europeans would have little choice but to attune their policy antennas to the East.

In summary, then, there appears to be an adequate military balance in Europe at present which can be sustained by equitable burden-sharing efforts and which ought to be sustained until there is either a negotiated mutual force reduction on both sides of the line that divides Europe or until the prospects for long-term European security permit a more acceptable solution to the problems of Germany and Berlin.

Those who disagree with this assessment ought at least to articulate clearly their premises and not merely accept at face value cliches such as the following:

NATO's superiority permits reduction;

The United States can reduce and the Europeans will increase;

NATO is so badly outnumbered that a greater imbalance won't hurt it;

Europe can defend itself—and if it won't, why should we?;

Europe will unite if the Americans will just simply get out;

There is no threat;

The Soviets don't use force any more (this has been heard much less frequently since the Czechoslovakian invasion).

The military balance in Europe is the underpinning of a political balance which is in the interest of the United States and Western Europe; and in turn, that balance is the basis on which hopes for a long-range security settlement must be based.

Possibilities of Mutual Force Reductions

In light of the political and technical arguments concerning the military balance in Europe, let us look at specific prospects for mutual force reductions.

For two years, NATO has been engaged in studies to develop guidelines for alternative possible models of mutual force reductions. A decision was made at the Reykjavik meeting of NATO Foreign Ministers in June 1968 to initiate a process leading to mutual force reductions, and the communique from that meeting called on the Soviet Union and other countries of Eastern Europe to join in this search for progress toward peace (See Appendix B).

Shelved because of lack of response from the Soviet Union and, of course, the invasion of Czechoslovakia, the idea now seems ripe for reopening in the European security context. NATO has reportedly accelerated its preparation of models, as part of a report to Ministers planned for the spring of 1970, to prepare a "realistic basis for active exploration at an early date." (See Appendix B.)

Earlier in this analysis it was noted how difficult are definitive judgments about the state of the present military balance and how complex the melange of considerations that affect the division of the burden on the Western side. Add the asymmetries in the East-West comparison, and the problem becomes still harder: How many Warsaw Pact units are equivalent to how many of NATO—given their differing size, organization, missions, equipment, and distance from home base? How does one American unit moved three thousand miles from the front compare with Russian units withdrawn only three hundred miles? What geographic areas should be included? Should the emphasis be on manpower or units or both? Should mutual withdrawals apply to ground forces only, or to air forces and navies as well? Should units merely be redeployed or should they be disbanded? How should qualitative comparisons be made between Eastern and Western forces? What about inspection and verification? Who should get the benefit of reductions within NATO? How would reductions be distributed within the Warsaw Pact? At what level—even of balanced and mutual reductions—does the military picture change qualitatively? Would NATO need a new strategic concept? And so on, almost indefinitely.

Recent years have seen a marked improvement in NATO's ability to tackle such problems on a balanced political-military basis and to subject them to systematic analysis; but the very number and complexity of the questions may make fully satisfactory answers hard to come by. The search will be long as well as difficult; yet, given the underlying assumption that the military balance is now adequate as a deterrent, it may be possible to shortcut the analytical approach by a broad political judgment leading to specific proposals.

The possibilities are limited in theory, of course, only by one's imagination. Accordingly, various European groups and individuals have developed various models for force reductions, both with and without demilitarized zones, denuclearization, all-European security pacts and guarantees, and other arms control features.[33] The troop reductions proposed range from token to "massive"—say, up to three quarters of present strengths in manpower. Since space precludes a detailed review and analysis of these ideas here, one must hazard an overall judgment: All of the plans for mutual troop withdrawals appear to depend upon an established detente mood on both sides of the dividing line and specifically upon a Russian willingness to markedly reduce the Soviet military posture in Eastern Europe.

For the reason discussed earlier, that is, the internal security requirement for these Russian forces, such a willingness seems remote at present. Yet it might, conceivably, grow slowly from a small start if signs of the dire consequences which some Soviet policy makers predict as a basis for their opposition did not in fact appear after the initial steps. But it has to be put down as wishful thinking that the Soviets would take the chance of a major withdrawal from their forward posture, even for the "reward" of major Western reductions; or that Ulbricht would acquiesce in a "substantial reduction" of the Soviet troops on which the stability of his regime largely depends. Then too, the more detailed models that have been advanced encounter all of the analytical uncertainties and geopolitical asymmetries noted earlier.

On balance, therefore, it seems best to cut the mutual-force-reductions suit to fit the available quantities of political cloth. One proposal, put forward here for illustrative purposes only, would combine a small start with gradualism—that is, carefully defined stages—and a focus, initially at least, on ground-force manpower only. Four stages might be envisaged:

Stage One would consist of **a small American reduction,** let us say up to a maximum of ten percent of the present American strength in Europe. (That strength, in terms of manpower, is currently about three hundred thousand men in round numbers:* two hundred thousand in the Seventh Army;

---

*This figure (about ten thousand men less than the official estimates) allows for minor administrative "streamlining," presumably without affecting combat units, in which the Pentagon is continuously engaged.

seventy thousand in the U.S. Air Force, Europe; and thirty thousand in the Sixth Fleet.) This pump-priming American reduction might either be offered as an earnest of good intentions at the formal opening of negotiations (at some risk of reducing the Pact's incentives for mutuality, however) or made conditional on agreement to implement Stages Two and Three. In either case, the United States and NATO would have to agree to make no additional reductions, pending implementation by the Pact of its undertakings, and to maintain their own force levels in the event that the Pact did not, in fact, reduce. (Some of the Atlantic Council's advisory committee members have different views on this approach.)[34] For each stage, the end-strength would be a "floor;" but it should also be a "ceiling," offered to the other side on a reciprocal basis to preclude buildups, possibly with an exception procedure to allow for the contingency of a major crisis. The West Europeans would thus be asked to maintain their own forces at present strengths and quality and allow the United States to take the first "slice" in Stage One, as a concession to burden sharing.

Stage Two would involve **a ten percent cut across the board** in all ground forces stationed in the Warsaw Pact's Northern Tier—East Germany, Poland, and Czechoslovakia—and in the West German-Benelux area of NATO. The majority of NATO cuts would be European, in view of the "US-only" nature of Stage One; but this need not exclude some further American withdrawals, perhaps on a limited dual-basing arrangement such as that which led to a thirty-five thousand man redeployment in 1968-1969.[35] Whether carried out in terms of units or manning levels, this is well within the "tolerance" of Warsaw Pact internal security requirements discussed above and should not affect the overall military balance. Verification would be accomplished, first, by exchange of certifications of actions taken (for example, "West German Second Division reduced to fifty percent manning," "Soviet Eleventh Guards Division withdrawn to Leningrad"); and second, by confirmation through national intelligence sources, which should be adequate for a fairly routine order-of-battle evaluation of this type. Arrangements could be made for follow-up checks as required, through bilateral diplomatic channels. While controversial, with some risks involved,[36] this method of verification might avoid the prickly issue of international inspection, which the Soviets invariably denounce as espionage. In view of the size of this troop reduction, Stage Two might be envisaged as a one-year program.

Stage Three would begin once both sides agreed that implementation of Stage Two had in fact been carried out. Here the aim would be **an additional fifteen percent reduction** in active ground-force manpower in all NATO and Warsaw Pact countries, each side taken as an aggregate, including American forces in Western Europe and Soviet forces in Eastern Europe. The actual strengths to be taken as the base point would have to be determined in the negotiations. Using the ISS figures given in Appendix A, the balance within the East and the West and between them could be roughly maintained after a reduction which, in this scheme, would total 243,000 men in NATO (of which one third could be American) and 271,000 men in Pact ground forces (of which nearly one half could be Russian). These mutual force reductions should bring a significant lowering of the military temperature in the European area. But NATO's military advisors will quickly point out that this plan may be too symmetrical, given the innate advantages of the Warsaw Pact (distance, surprise, etc.), despite the fact that the percentage approach calls for larger reductions in Eastern forces than in NATO and by the Soviet Union than by the United States. However, the West can probably afford the risks inherent in these three stages, and therefore should postpone the question of asymmetry until the presumably better environment in Stage Four. This simple approach allows each side to organize and deploy its remaining forces as it sees fit, thus avoiding the dilemma of more comprehensive schemes: namely, that mutual force reductions cannot begin until an agreement is reached (which is rarely feasible) on the totality of forces in the military balance.

Stage Four: At the end of, say, a two-year program for Stage Three, detailed East-West negotiations should begin for a final ceiling and for the steps to reach it on both sides. Although one tends to think of a ceiling vis-à-vis the East and a floor within NATO, the Soviets undoubtedly have an interest in the latter too, though they cannot admit it, for the American presence gives them a sense of stability and a hedge against the unknown future of European politics. Depending on the political climate, the eventual level of manpower on each side might be as much as one third below that reached at the end of Stage Three. Also, air and naval forces should be included for the first time at this point. Of course, if understandings on the growing Soviet naval threat to NATO in the Mediterranean can be reached sooner as a separate matter, so much the better. This challenge has increased rather dramatically in the last three years in terms of the Russian presence there; but, as with the air force component, it is too difficult to establish equivalencies, given differing functions and the greater mobility of naval forces in contrast to land forces. Thus, one possible approach for Stage Four would involve limiting manpower—the common denominator of all weapons systems—deployed within a defined area, whether soldiers, sailors, or airmen.

In Stage Four both sides would have to conduct fairly detailed reviews of the strategies, missions, and deployments of their remaining forces. In that regard, there are too many variables for discussion here as part of this proposal, beyond noting that whereas the Warsaw Pact might get through

Stage Three within the assumed limitations of their internal security needs in Eastern Europe, Stage Four would go beyond them. On the NATO side, even to get through Stage Two might require some restructuring of forces—perhaps with smaller but better and more mobile counterattacking forces, supplemented by light and inexpensive "forward-defense" units (to provide the screening and delaying function), as well as ready and mobilizable reserves to augment NATO's posture in the event of a renewed crisis. This restructuring of NATO forces could be carried out within the present overall strategy of "assured response and flexible escalation,"[37] should it become necessary; and there are some good arguments which can be made for it on the grounds of cost-effectiveness, quite apart from mutual force reductions.

Stage Four would involve rethinking the entire basis of European defense, the requirements of deterrence, and the role of nuclear weapons in light of the then existing strategic arms situation and the state of genuine detente in Europe. Hard as this rethinking might be, it would doubtless be easier to consider once the first three stages had been completed satisfactorily. Moreover, West Europeans might by then have made further progress in pooling some of their armaments and logistics functions in order to achieve the necessary economy of scale for more efficient use of lesser military resources.[38]

There are many forums through which any such plan for mutual force reductions could be explored and negotiated; and one of them could be a European security conference. But the rather extensive intramural discussions that would have to precede East-West talks might make the use of a large gathering difficult. A better approach might be preliminary explorations by one or more individual governments, as authorized by NATO and the Warsaw Pact. Alternatively, NATO's Secretary General could be authorized to make tentative soundings with his opposite number (who, on the civilian side, is a Soviet foreign office functionary) and in Warsaw Pact capitals.

This possibility is a particularly attractive one; for the incumbent on NATO's side, Manlio Brosio, is one of the West's most experienced diplomats. He has served as Italian Ambassador in Washington, Moscow, London, and Paris, and he commands great respect for his objectivity and his ability to act for the whole Alliance.

The flaws in this otherwise sensible proposal for mutual force reductions are, first, that the East might not want to discuss so sensitive a subject with the head of the alliance they ostensibly would like to see abolished; but refusal to do so would put them in a difficult propaganda position. This sensitivity may be behind some recent indications of Russian interest; but it is too soon to rule out a genuine desire for mutual and balanced force reductions.[39]

Second, the French remain adamantly opposed to any bloc-to-bloc diplomacy, on the grounds that only sovereign governments, and not alliances, conduct foreign policy. But there is a way around this latter problem. Since French forces have been withdrawn from NATO, they would not—or need not—be included in the proposal. It could then be handled as a military-planning matter by NATO's Defense Planning Committee (DPC), from which an "exploratory" mandate for Secretary General Brosio might derive. This group evolved constitutionally from the North Atlantic Council and acts as a board of directors to deal with matters concerning NATO's integrated defenses, in which France has chosen to take no part. This Alliance legacy from General de Gaulle could justly be employed to surmount the "no bloc-to-bloc" legacy which he left the Quai.

A Western initiative along these lines (whether or not involving the Secretary General) or even the same substantive proposal could very well be made at the NATO Ministerial meetings to be held this spring in Rome. Exploratory discussions of mutual force reductions could be a useful bellwether with respect to the value of an East-West conference on European security, especially if a relatively simple and modest (and therefore more practical) offer of this general type were involved.

Other Security Questions

Mutual force reductions have been treated here in terms of conventional armaments, primarily ground forces, because that is the way the concept has been dealt with in the context of the European security problem. But they are only half, albeit a vital half, of the overall military balance, the other part of which involves nuclear weapons.

"Tactical" Nuclear Weapons and SALT

The United States and Russia have at last gotten to the table to begin discussions of "strategic arms limitation." President Johnson was on the point of announcing discussions on August 20, 1968, the day Soviet tanks rolled into Czechoslovakia. The meeting was shelved—reluctantly it seems—because of that event. After a decent period of mourning, the matter was reopened. This time it was the Russians who seemed uncomfortable, reportedly owing to internal disagreements and the prospect of simultaneously holding talks with China on border disputes. But after the usual difficulties of selecting a mutually acceptable site, the first sessions of SALT, the currently fashionable acronym for "strategic arms limitation talks," got underway in Helsinki in November 1969.[40] These meetings, according to the sparse information made public, were purely exploratory, with no substantive proposals made on either side. Each presumably explained its thinking about such questions as the distinction between strategic arms and other weapons systems, various aspects of stability, and ways of avoiding dangerous miscalculations.

It is uncertain, at best, whether each side has really clarified its perceptions of the other side's objectives, evaluations of the current strategic balance, and mirror image of its opponent's perceptions.* Not until the talks resume in April 1970 will it be possible to tell whether any agreement seems possible and what its scope and significance might be. In a discussion of the immediate issue of European security, therefore, it is tempting to dismiss strategic arms limitation on a wait-and-see basis. But there is too close a connection between the two subjects to do so. For one thing, the simple fact that the two superpowers are negotiating with each other on such a vital security issue is a political event of no minor significance. Furthermore, to some nervous Europeans, East and West, and to a few theorists of international relations, the mere process smacks of condominum or even hegemony with respect to Europe.

Fortunately, most observers recognize that whatever their antagonisms, the United States and Russia share a common responsibility for survival which they do not share in the same way with any third state. Of course, this is because only these two nations currently possess the physical power to destroy each other as viable societies—even after being attacked first.

For the West, at least, there is nothing incompatible between negotiations to reduce the costs and dangers of the nuclear arms race and the maintenance of an alliance system which is based on a perceived challenge from the other superpower and its allies and which stabilizes the political balance between "different social systems," as the Russians say. The United States has reportedly made a major effort to consult fully and in advance with its NATO partners. President Nixon pledged himself to continue to discuss the various opinions with our allies, since he considers "our security inseparable from theirs."[41]

In the East, Khrushchev recognized in the early 1960's that the conflict with capitalism had to be conducted below the nuclear threshold; but there are probably tensions within a Soviet hierarchy which has ideological constraints that make it reluctant to accept limitations on its power by agreement with its enemies. And there may be fear that the mere appearance of such an agreement, quite apart from the reality, could exert counter-

---

*To illustrate the mirror-image effect of perceptions, imagine that State A seeks a balance—and believes one exists. State B may also seek a balance—and believes it exists. But agreement may still be impossible if B thinks that A really wants, and is trying to get, superiority or if B thinks that A believes itself behind and so will undertake a major catch-up effort in its strategic forces.

pressures against the level of tension, internal and external, needed to hold the Soviet system together. Some Kremlin-watchers believe that the maneuverings now underway for a Party congress in 1970 may preface a change in Soviet leadership, as similar maneuverings have frequently done in the past. If so, the future of SALT is even more cloudy.

Foreign Minister Gromyko's June 1968 report to the Supreme Soviet rationalized the Russian willingness to start SALT by explaining that "there are actions in international affairs that are difficult to classify as purely foreign policy or purely ideological actions. More often than not, they are a combination of the two. . . .the foreign-policy activities of governments today are marked by, and interwoven with the clash of ideologists."[42]

Most American officials rightly believe that strategic arms limitation is important and its ultimate logic unavoidable. But there are three important respects in which the American point of view differs from the West European—and even more so, presumably, from the Russian. First, it is an American tradition to "say what one means and to mean what one says." Not so in much of the world's diplomacy; why something is said is often believed to be more important than what is said, and motives are suspect in direct proportion to the significance of the subject. The more candid the Americans are about their interests, the greater the Russian suspicion that something is being "put on."

Second, America's unique global position makes it possible to put forward genuinely balanced, objective proposals. But these are not received objectively in any society where the dialectical tradition is strong, as in Russia. There, one bargains by asking the impossibly high price; one eventually compromises only after receiving a ridiculously low counter-offer.

And third, there is the factor of lead time. Only in the last decade has American thinking reached the sophisticated level of asking about the uses of military power in the nuclear age and thereby recognized the nonutility of open-ended arms expansion. Only recently has the notion of relative security become accepted. And even today, the interaction of political perceptions, of deterrence and defense, and of offensive and defensive strategic systems is not widely or fully understood. There are certainly some Russians who understand these complex mechanics very well. But not so the dominant Soviet military men, many of whom are strategic primitives, so to speak. They regard international political power as an end; the greater the military strength they have in absolute terms, the greater their power—Q.E.D. Thus, they are several years behind their Western counterparts in the understanding of arms control, as indeed they have been in their comprehension of nuclear strategy.

SALT may therefore prove to be a dialogue between the hard of hearing and the deaf. And the critical question is how much momentum in the Soviet strategic buildup the United States can tolerate—especially with the Russian deployment of the SS-9 and SS-11 missiles as major counterforce weapons—while waiting for Soviet leaders to catch up in their strategic thinking, before the United States reacts with a combination of MIRV's, ABM's, and completely new strategic systems.

Suppose, nevertheless, that SALT does progress to the point of discussing actual systems and bargaining about limiting them. Here is where the word "strategic" becomes critical. A weapons system can be defined in terms of its **mission** (counter-city or counterforce), its **range** (short, long, or medium), its **size** (kilotons or megatons), and its **target** (battlefield, interdiction, or enemy homeland).

There are, according to official American statements, over seven thousand American nuclear warheads in Europe. Most of them are classified by the United States as "tactical." But some of them can be delivered to targets in Russia, as well as to forces in the "engaged battle area" or in Eastern Europe. The Russians have some seven hundred medium- and intermediate-range ballistic missles (MRBM's and IRBM's) aimed at Western Europe, plus hundreds of nuclear-capable short-range rockets. There have even been press reports[43] that some ICBM's are now being deployed in missile complexes previously containing only MRBM's.* Nevertheless, medium-range missiles are surely strategic to Western Europe; and some of the American systems based in Europe may be so classified by the Russians—however tactical they may seem in Washington.

The point is that sooner or later "strategic arms talks" may begin to affect the people in the launching or target areas of systems whose classification is ambiguous. This will face the United States—and NATO—with important tests of sincerity about consultation. If the United States were to insist on a reduction of Soviet medium-range ballistic missiles (MRBM's), then the Russians might well counter with a request for reduction of NATO's tactical nuclear stockpiles, many of which exist for the direct support of allied forces. And in this area, unlike the area of mutual reductions of ground forces, "verification" is almost impossible, even conceptually. Both sides regard the numbers, types, and locations of their nuclear weapons as their most vital secrets.

---

*The Soviets may thus try to obtain "dual-capability" systems which can be used against either the United States or Western Europe. If so, this might be related to the SALT distinction between strategic arms and other systems, either to gain from the ambiguity during any negotiations or to try to produce problems for the United States in NATO.

The very complexity of this issue—and the importance of detailed NATO participation on the Western side (the degree to which the Soviets consult their allies on matters of strategy is unknown)—makes it appear unsuitable for inclusion on the agenda of an East-West European security conference. But as the next logical extension of SALT, the question of tactical nuclear weapons remains high on the list of European security issues. The United States is certainly not going to talk with the Russians about British or French forces, but these too have some relevance to the overall East-West strategic picture.

Consequently, the prospect of superpower negotiations on strategic arms will inevitably give rise to a desire, in both East and West Europe, to be seen doing something about the nuclear armaments of primary relevance to Europe. And an East-West security conference would doubtless be a forum for ventilating, even if not resolving, this desire. To the extent that the Soviet Union was compelled thereby to initiate the kind of frank discussions within the Warsaw Pact which NATO has come to expect with the United States, the interests of all might be advanced.

However, the Warsaw Pact's propaganda line until now has called for denuclearizing only Western Europe, particularly West Germany. It calls, for example, for an atom-free zone or a freeze on nuclear weapons, and nothing is said about Russian MRBM's aimed at the zone from outside it. These weapons, as Khrushchev often reminded us, make Western Europe Russia's hostage. Consequently, the Soviet Union seems unlikely to negotiate about these Russian-based missiles even with its allies, let alone in a large East-West forum.

On balance then, the relationship between SALT and nuclear systems in Europe seems best worked out first within each side, and then by specialized negotiations between them, rather than in the setting of a major East-West conference.

Counter-Surprise and Confidence-Building Measures

Discussion of measures to avoid surprise attack and miscalculation takes one back to the days of the "spirit of Geneva" and the Eisenhower Administration of the 1950's. The United States put forward then a number of ideas—including the open-skies proposal—which have not led to any serious response from the other side. Development of what the press calls spy satellites may have overtaken the original open-skies idea; and, of course, a limited nuclear test moratorium (a precursor to the atmospheric test ban) did flow from the Geneva and Camp David discussions.

In European-security terms, however, the counter-surprise and confidence-building concept has usually taken the form of proposals for (1) the exchange of observers; (2) the establishment of overlapping radar/observation posts, i.e., by each side in the other's territory; and (3) mutual notification of exercises and maneuvers. And in its December 1969 declaration, NATO called for further studies of such measures, which might accompany or follow mutual and balanced force reductions. (See Appendix B.)

The first proposal already exists in the so-called Military Liaison Missions, which, as has been mentioned, have been operating in both parts of Germany since the Potsdam Conference of 1945. Over the years, the Soviets have developed a technique of restricted zones for military maneuvers—often covering large areas of East Germany—from which Western teams are excluded. And the West has frequently retaliated in kind. It seems unlikely that the East Germans and Russians would agree in advance to forswear this practice, and once access is sharply limited, the utility of expanding the observer system seems questionable.

The second measure has merit in principle; each side could maintain a series of fixed posts or radar stations (and, of course, constant communications with its own side) far enough within the territory of its adversary on the other side of the border to have early warning of any major buildup of forces.[44] But nothing in Soviet behavior to date suggests that the idea would be any more tolerable than international inspection, which Russia has always flatly refused.

The third proposal, notification of exercises, has not been discussed in detail and could conceivably be put on the agenda of a European security conference. The main benefit would be in confidence building, since major maneuvers are scheduled far in advance and follow seasonal and training cycles well-known to the intelligence agencies of both sides. But even an agreement to give formal notice of exercises in advance would not prevent the use of a military maneuver as the cover for an invasion buildup—like the ruse which the Soviets and their Warsaw Pact allies used in their invasion of Czechoslovakia. A military engagement might also arise out of an overreaction to one side's maneuvers. So this confidence-building measure would be of limited effect in preventing "accidental conflict," since neither side could afford to trust completely the schedule it received. Furthermore, both sides might also be reluctant to tie their hands in advance, since training, weather, and international conditions often call for last-minute changes in a long-planned maneuver.

These ideas could, of course, be explored in an international security meeting, but they would also seem to be the legitimate business of the Eighteen National Disarmament Conference (ENDC) at Geneva, in which the United States and the Soviet Union, as well as other NATO and Warsaw Pact members, take part.

Renunciations of Force and Nonagression Pacts

That renunciation of force can be regarded as an issue may come as a surprise to a reader of the United Nations Charter, who might be forgiven for thinking that the matter had been settled—to the extent that solemn obligations can settle anything—back in 1945 by Article 2, paragraph 4, which reads:

> All Members. . . .shall refrain in their international relations from the threat or use of force against the territorial integrity or political independence of any state, or in any other manner inconsistent with the Purposes of the United Nations.

Part of the problem is that neither West nor East Germany is a member of the United Nations. A specific mutual renunciation of force with the Soviet Union would therefore fill a lacuna in the network of international legal obligations, and presumably add a further handicap to any German effort to seek readjustment of the de facto frontiers about which even an indirect threat of force might be implied. But as Willy Brandt said in a Bundestag debate while he was Foreign Minister of the Grand Coalition,

> We have clearly expressed our readiness to formulate in binding terms the renunciation of the application of force and the threat of force vis-à-vis all East European partners. . .and vis-à-vis the other part of Germany.[45]

Brandt characterized renunciation of force as the "corner-stone of our European and East European policy."

Since the West prefers to de-emphasize the political and economic significance of frontiers, at least in the iron curtain sense, stressing their inviolability may be the preferred approach.

For its part, the Soviet Union prefers to cite Articles 53 and 107, which except from United Nations' jurisdiction measures against any "enemy state," meaning Germany, in this case. On more than one occasion, the Soviet Union has made ominous public references to these provisions in the context of alleged German revanchism.

One quid pro quo which the West might seek, therefore, is a formal recognition by the U.S.S.R. that these aspects of what the Charter calls transitional security arrangements have been overtaken by events.

But there is another troublesome aspect. The Soviet invasion of Czechoslovakia not only flagrantly violated the previously quoted provision of Article 2 about refraining from the use of force but it also transgressed the 1966 Bucharest communique of the Warsaw Pact itself. (See Appendix C.) At Rumanian insistence, the call for a European security conference at that meeting was based on principles of "independence and national sovereignty, non-interference in internal affairs and the renunciation of any kind of discrimination and pressures aimed against other countries." This theme has not been stressed in the post-Czechoslovakia renewals of calls for a conference.

But a new exegesis, the Brezhnev Doctrine, has since entered the international lexicon of Communism. This doctrine of a "socialist commonwealth" was of course an ex post facto justification for Soviet operations in Czechoslovakia. In a rather chilling article entitled "Sovereignty and International Duties," *Pravda* spelled out this doctrine a month after the invasion:

> The sovereignty of each socialist country cannot be opposed to the interests of the socialist world, and the interests of the world revolutionary movement. Formal observance of the freedom of self-determination of a nation in that concrete situation which arose in Czechoslovakia would mean freedom of "self-determination" not for the popular masses, the working people, but for their enemies. One must not lose a class approach beneath arguments of a formal juridical character. Such a [bourgeois] approach to the question of sovereignty means that, for example, the progressive forces of the world would not be able to come out against the revival of neo-Nazism in the Federal Republic of Germany, against the actions of the butchers Franco and Salazar, against reactionary, arbitrary actions of "black colonels" in Greece because this is "the internal affair" of "sovereign" states.[46]

The double standard is, of course, not new to Communism. *Pravda* duly quoted Lenin's dictum that "each man must choose between joining our side or taking the other side. Any attempt to avoid taking sides in this issue must end in fiasco." But even Europe's Communists were shocked. As one put it,

> Never has the world been made to understand the purpose of the Warsaw Pact is to maintain a specific social level in its members' regimes. Hence the surprise of the world upon learning that the leading member-states have the right of intervention in the internal affairs of other members not excluding military intervention. If this right exists, then what is involved is not a defensive pact but a mechanism resembling the Holy Alliance, a notorious policeman in Europe after the fall of Napoleon.[47]

At its special meeting in November 1968, the NATO Ministers specifically rejected this notion of limited sovereignty and a right of intervention within the "Socialist Commonwealth;"* and they gave a veiled warning that serious international consequences would flow from any repetition of Czechoslovakia, say, against Rumania.

---

*The NATO communique states: "The contention of the Soviet leadership that there exists a right of intervention in the affairs of other states deemed to be within a so-called 'Socialist Commonwealth' runs counter to the basic principles of the United Nations Charter, is dangerous to European security, and has inevitably aroused grave anxieties." Secretary of State Rogers has also commented on this impediment to detente in Europe. (See Chapter 3.)

Given the deep ideological roots suggested by the *Pravda* quotation, it would be unrealistic to expect any overt Russian retraction of the Brezhnev Doctrine, which is the Soviet's clear warning to their satellites not to get out of step. But equally, the West cannot afford to ignore the only recent use of force in Europe and then go on to exchange declarations which, by implication, tacitly treat that doctrine as some sort of exception to the "non-use of force" principle. One possible advantage of an East-West security conference would be to get the Soviet Union on the record once again in support of the nonagression principle in a way which would be helpful to the East Europeans in resisting future Soviet pressures, perhaps along the lines of the "Rumanian clause" of the Bucharest declaration. But it is unclear at best how the ghost of the Brezhnev Doctrine could be laid to rest in any discussion of the principle in a European security conference.

Meanwhile, West Germany continues bilateral discussions of mutual force renunciations with East Germany, Poland, and the Soviet Union; but the peculiarities of the German question mean that the Brezhnev Doctrine is not involved in this unique East-West context, since the application of any West Germany-East European mutual force reduction would be bilateral.

As the cornerstone of the *Ostpolitik* of both the Grand Coalition and the Socialist-Free Democrat coalition, renunciation of force really serves an essentially procedural purpose, aside of course, from atmospheric side effects. For it defines a permissible subject for German negotiations on an individual basis with the Czechs and Poles, as well as with the East Germans and Russians, posing delicate problems of Communist diplomatic coordination.[48] Thus, it may be an opening wedge for genuinely substantive negotiations on, for example, Germany's external boundaries with Poland and Czechoslovakia—on the Oder-Neisse line and the complexities of the Munich Agreement of 1938 (which accepted Hitler's aggression against Czechoslovakia). All concerned agree that the Munich Agreement is invalid, but the precise Soviet formulation of *ab initio* invalidity raises legal complications involving international claims.[49]

The press coverage of *Ostpolitik* since December 1969 gives the reader an impression of frenetic activity and rapid, perhaps even dramatic, change. The fact of the matter is that the diplomats concerned anticipate a long and arduous series of negotiations, with pauses for reconsideration and coordination in both East and West and with an outcome which is uncertain at best. A good case can be made, therefore, that the quieter this diplomacy, the better. But avoidance of press sensationalism is not prominent among Bonn's virtues—especially on a matter which not only is one of such deep interest to all Germans and, indeed, to all members of NATO but also is one of the key yardsticks of performance for the first Socialist government in Germany since the days of the Weimar Republic.

Paralleling the notion of renouncing the use of force is a sporadic call in Warsaw Pact propaganda for an exchange of nonagression pacts with NATO. This has become a standard item on a menu which also lists liquidation of foreign military bases, withdrawal of "foreign" forces (redefined as "non European" forces, after the 1968 Czechoslovakian invasion), and recognition of two German states. It is advertised as the first step toward the dissolution of the two military blocs. How seriously the Russians—as the victims in 1941 of one of the most infamous nonagression pacts in history—take this as a form of security can only be speculated. It was, however, featured as an agenda item in the Warsaw Pact's call for an East-West security conference in October 1969 (See Appendix C); but as has been mentioned, the East Europeans have nevertheless also begun a series of bilateral negotiations with Bonn on renunciations of force. Accordingly, a nonaggression pact might be a way to get around the Brezhnev Doctrine, the major impediment to force renunciations—in the event that such "trimmings" should prove important to the packaging of substantive agreements, for example, on mutual force reductions.

Trade, Cultural, and Scientific Contacts

Western nations have had to face the fact that whether they like it or not, the Communist system will remain installed in Eastern Europe for a long time to come and that no one is willing to risk nuclear war to "roll back" the iron curtain. The essentially propagandistic nature of "liberation" was clearly revealed by Western inaction during the Hungarian revolt of 1956—when there were at least some active options which could have been adopted.

That being the fact, and given a Western determination to maintain the present dividing line in Europe against forcible change from the East, attention quite naturally focuses on the politics of penetrating the iron curtain by osmosis. The implicit assumption is not that the Eastern regime would thereby be subverted, although this motive is often charged by the other side, but rather that the pace of internal change could be speeded up by contacts of various kinds and that the "embourgeoisification" of people in the East would inevitably permit a relaxation of both internal and external tensions. During discussions on trade controls, some West Europeans have sometimes used the colorful argument that "a fat Communist is less dangerous than a hungry one"—although it is sometimes fair to wonder whether the real appetite has not been on the part of the West's own export industry.

Starting in the mid-1950's, cultural exchanges, trade fairs, and scientific contacts have represented a sublimated outlet for the East-West stalemate on political and military security issues. Zbigniew Brzezinski describes the process in this way:

> The European partition is slowly being undone in the cultural and economic realms. Step by step, closer links between Western and Eastern Europe are being forged, although the process has been meeting with some resistance from both sides. Broadly speaking, the East European governments favor dismantling the Iron Curtain rapidly in the economic field while lifting it only very gradually in the social.[50]

The West, on the other hand, is conservative about opening the trade doors too widely but is seeking more cultural and social access. Understandably, the East is trying to maximize its economic and technological gains at minimum risk of political contamination.

The Communist attitude toward "capitalistic" international arrangements such as the General Agreement on Tariffs and Trade (GATT) has been cool, to say the least; for the rules were not designed for the type of state trading done by members of COMECON (Council of Mutual Economic Assistance) in Eastern Europe. Yugoslavia acceded to GATT in 1966, after successful experimentation with decentralization of trading, and Poland became a full member in 1967—the first to do so under centrally planned foreign trade arrangements. Progress on Rumania's application was held up by the invasion of Czechoslovakia.[51]

A similar pattern of propaganda attacks, studied indifference, and finally, pragmatic adjustments, characterizes the Communist attitude toward the European Common Market. Thus far, trade has been worked out through ad hoc bilateral arrangements with individual members of the EEC. But under EEC rules these agreements must be phased out by January 1973, and they will eventually be replaced by a common commercial policy toward the Communist countries. The first formal commercial treaty—a three year nonpreferential, nondiscriminatory pact between the Common Market and Yugoslavia—has just been signed.[52]

It is important to keep in mind the fact that the total free-world trade with Communist countries has been running at about four percent or less of total world trade for both imports and exports. Western Europe's trade with Russia and Eastern Europe was about five percent of total exports (four billion seven hundred million dollars out of ninety-two billion) and just under five percent for imports (four billion eight hundred million dollars out of one hundred one billion).[53] But it has been growing from year to year, although it is not yet a major factor in the international commercial transactions of either side. United States competitive interests in East-West trade may be growing too, for America's relatively high rate of inflation continues to price American goods out of many foreign markets. The reversal from a U.S.

surplus of exports over imports to a deficit can in time become serious in a political as well as a financial sense. If adequate forms of payments could be devised, it might be in the American interest to seek a large-scale increase in exports of farm machinery and related types of goods to Russia and Eastern Europe.

What may be more significant in the long run are the large package deals involving the use of natural gas as a bartering item.[54] This transaction illustrates a classic problem in East-West trade: the shortage of goods and financing in the East. Traditionally, Eastern Europe was regarded as Western Europe's breadbasket or, more pejoratively, its economic back yard. Although there is still substantial trade in commodities, the East lacks both the hard currency and the high-quality manufactured products needed to compete in Western markets. Thus, from an ideal standpoint, the East would like to import advanced technology and capital goods, ranging from machine tools to complete factories, with which to produce and export machinery and finished items to the less developed world in exchange for raw materials. These can then be transshipped or processed for sale in the West. But even to finance this triangular trade pattern, the East must rely on long-term credits. This gives the West some potential leverage, if it can agree on general guidelines to govern such credit lines so as to avoid a competitive scramble. Efforts toward such agreement in NATO and in the OECD have had some success but have proved difficult at best.

Most of the testimony before Congress in recent years has supported the idea that nonstrategic trade does serve a bridge-building function and encourages the Eastern economies in "peaceful directions."[55] But despite Administration support, measures to permit extension of most-favored-nation treatment to members of the Eastern bloc have encountered Congressional roadblocks.[56] The OECD has undertaken specific studies of the trade effects of economic reforms in Eastern Europe, and the United Nations Economic Commission for Europe provides a forum for East-West discussion of such key issues as state trading and most-favored-nation treatment. Thus, in summary, despite the importance of trade as one factor in improving East-West relations, there are inherent market limits and numerous practical problems on which several organizations—at least one combining both OECD and COMECON members—are active already. It is not readily apparent, therefore, that a European security conference could make any useful contribution on matters of trade, beyond very general exhortations. The Communist countries could and probably would use the occasion to mount a propaganda attack on the West's remaining strategic-trade controls, which include certain areas of advanced technology (computers and electronics, for example) of considerable military importance.

Since the East's practical interest in economic matters leads them to give priority to business visitors, the kinds of personal contacts made through trade channels can be significant in widening the social and political horizons of the elites in Eastern Europe. For example, Roswell Garst, a hybrid corn expert from Iowa, visited with Chairman Khrushchev personally on four different occasions, as well as with Mikoyan and numerous leaders in Eastern Europe.[57] Scientific visitors—especially ones likely to be helpful to Soviet science—also tend to receive special treatment. The same is true, in principle at least, of cultural and tourist travel, although to a lesser degree, since tourists in Russia have much more restricted access to leadership elements, and even the general population are under strong disincentives to friendliness with Westerners.

Here again, statistics are a measure of the realities. Italy and Spain have some twenty-eight million and sixteen million visitors per year, respectively, and Yugoslavia has from three to four million. By contrast, the Soviet Union has less than two million, and all the other Eastern European countries combined have less than Austria and Switzerland. The same disparity exists in external travel; for example, French travellers to other European countries total over twelve million—five times the number of travellers from Eastern Europe.[58]

Despite the growth of travel to Eastern Europe in recent years, stimulated mainly by special rates to attract foreign currency, East-West contacts through travel and student exchanges must be regarded as a very gradual and long-term means of liberalizing the East. This is not to suggest that this travel is unimportant, for such contacts are one of the few means by which people in the Eastern countries are exposed to information and ideas other than the Party line. But it is not clear whether a formal East-West conference could do much to increase either tourist or cultural exchanges, which are tightly controlled by the East and, as with trade, dealt with in multilateral bodies, such as UNESCO, or on a bilateral basis. For example, the United States and the Soviet Union recently signed their seventh cultural exchange agreement covering 1970-1971. The student and faculty exchanges will be raised from forty to three hundred; and the performing arts groups from three to five.[59] At best, an additional international conference would provide a forum in which the West could demonstrate its genuine and nonexploitative interest in the expansion of contacts between "peoples of different social systems," and thus, indirectly at least, bring pressure to bear on the East for a widening of the crack in its door.

With respect to science, a case can be made that the informal and specialized exchanges taking place, in the Pugwash conferences, for example, have succeeded in opening bridges and allowing at least some Russians to share American perspectives on arms control, precisely because they were not large, official gatherings. Here, too, the trade-off is between the East's desire for access to applied science—although the West has an interest going beyond idle curiosity in Soviet scientific developments—and the West's hope to establish a framework of understanding for the political implications of science. One new field in which to explore such implications (in addition, of course, to arms control) is that of ecology and the world environment. This appears to have a unique promise, by virtue of its long-run importance and its noncontroversial nature; thus, it seems to deserve special attention. (See Chapter 6.)

In summary, although these several areas cannot be said to bear directly on European security issues, they can and do affect both the diplomatic climate within which political bargaining takes place and the long-range perceptions of both East and West. For this reason, there is at least an indirect tie to the security conference proposal—and indeed the trade aspects have been specifically included on the agenda proposed at the Prague meeting of the Warsaw Pact in October 1969. (See Appendix C.) Yet, it seems doubtful whether the "atmospheric" impact of a conference on the hard questions of ways and means to improve trade and contacts would by itself justify an East-West conference. There are important rivalries within Eastern Europe: for example, resentment of East Germany's special trade relationship with West Germany. This "interzonal trade" virtually makes East Germany a member of the European Common Market with respect to some important privileges. "Why," ask the Czechs and Poles, "should Ulbricht get these economic benefits, even while his political hard line keeps us from fruitful contact with the West?" But such internal conflicts of interest are unlikely to be allowed to surface in an East-West conference.

Thus, on balance, one must be doubtful of the value of a major new East-West security conference environment for these "issues"—though not pessimistic about the value of promoting trade, cultural, and scientific exchanges in their own right.

5 Motivations and Procedures: Timing, Tactics, and Tests of Sincerity

In evaluating the pros and cons of a conference on European security from the Western point of view, it is important to clarify further the key question of Soviet motivations in the light of the issues and their history discussed previously. Do the Soviets merely want to ratify the present division of Europe? Or is there some genuine interest in ending it? Proposals for all-European conferences or congresses, it should be recalled, have played a featured, if periodic, role in Soviet diplomacy since World War II. Among the Soviet foreign policy objectives which most Western observers consider standard are the following:

First, to consolidate the Soviet position and legitimacy in Eastern Europe.

Second, to legalize the division of Germany and obtain diplomatic recognition for the German Democratic Republic plus international acceptance of Germany's borders.

Third, to create divisions between NATO members and generally to undermine the NATO alliance.

Fourth, to reduce the influence of the United States in, and promote American disengagement from, Europe (however, many observers find that the Soviets also have some stake in the stability provided by the American presence).

Fifth, to denuclearize Central Europe and particularly to bar the Federal Republic from access to nuclear weapons in any form.

Sixth, to retard the process of West European political, economic, and social unification—particularly, to inhibit the growth of the European Economic Community and to block membership of the United Kingdom.

(One observer has speculated about a possible Communist follow-up to a Gaullist suggestion—obviously aimed at Britain—that the EEC should reach a security and cooperation agreement with COMECON before admitting new members.)[1]

Seventh, to undermine Western controls on strategic trade with the Soviet Union and Eastern Europe.

Eighth, to promote left-center movements, "peace" groups, and the appeal of "neutrality" in Western Europe and to advance the influence of western Communist parties.

Ninth, to regain Soviet leadership in and control of the international Communist movement, particularly in the face of rival claims from the Peoples' Republic of China.

Some or all of these elements are contained in one or more versions of the European security conference proposal. And some, to be sure, are furthered merely in the proposing. It is tempting, therefore, to dismiss the current East European initiative as a purely propaganda exercise and a trap for the West.[2] Indeed, there are some who so view it; at least one expert prefers to call it a European suicide conference. Nevertheless, despite the large helpings of propaganda and political tactics in the proposal, an objective evaluation must consider whether there are "genuine and legitimate" Soviet motivations for seeking a European security settlement.

One such factor is undoubtedly the growing concern over the confrontation with Communist China. Given the uncertain course of that conflict, it would be reasonable for the Soviet Union to seek to secure its rear, that is, Eastern Europe and the border with Western Europe; for this would not only make it easier to transfer military resources from Western Russia to Asian Russia but might also gather support in Eastern Europe for any ideological showdown the Soviets might have with Communist China. Moreover, the avoidance of a two-front war, in the political sense, could strengthen the Soviet bargaining position for dealing with China.

A second legitimate factor in Soviet motivations might be internal economic pressures against the current high rate of defense spending (estimated to be nine percent of the Soviet gross national product), not only on strategic forces—this being a probable factor in the Soviet decision to undertake SALT—but also on general-purpose forces, involving some three million men. Such pressures certainly exist. How strong they are—given an economy which is relatively stagnant in terms of past performance and given considerable consumer pressures for a higher standard of living—is a matter on which experts can and do differ.* It is also unclear how much influence on

---

*While still increasing, the rate of economic growth is believed by Western experts to be the lowest in several years, and the economy has structural problems involving the role of the Party, the degree of centralization, and the use of market factors in pricing. Debates continue over the need for, and type of, basic reforms to be made in the Soviet economic system.

foreign and defense policy decisions various factions have in the Soviet power structure.[3] Then, too, there is a genuine need in Eastern Europe, including the U.S.S.R., for Western trade, technology, and credits.

The East is well aware of the potential availability of Western capital surpluses—especially in Germany—which are seeking foreign markets, and of the interest of Western businessmen in the type of arrangement which Fiat recently made to construct an entire auto-manufacturing plant in the Soviet Union or in the Russo-German natural-gas-pipeline agreement. A security settlement with the West—or an appearance of one—would clearly enhance the availability and internal acceptability of such trade and credits; and it could further undermine the remaining Western controls on certain categories of strategic materials, for example in the electronics and computer area, where the Russians lag severely behind the West in technology.

It is also possible that new elements of realism are beginning to influence Soviet assessments. For example, they probably recognize that NATO, having successfully passed 1969, the twenty-year milestone,* has now come of age, and that it has surmounted the French defection from the military side of the Alliance. NATO has worked out a modus vivendi with the French, and there is no sign that the Alliance will wither away, for the next several years at least.

Coupled with signs of progress in the European Economic Community, this could lead the Soviets to decide to "contain" the West politically rather than use periodic confrontations and propaganda—and perhaps even to follow the expanded-contacts rationale discussed in the preceding chapter. Moreover, one might speculate that the invasion of Czechoslovakia was—for at least the younger generation of Russians—what Vietnam has become to their counterparts in the United States. But this must remain speculation, for the opportunities for knowledge and dissent remain severely restricted in the Soviet Union.

Finally, it is possible that the Soviet leadership has decided to "multilateralize" the problems of European security, as a way of bringing to bear concerns in Eastern Europe, and to a lesser degree in the West, about the Federal Republic's economic strength and *Ostpolitik*. Perhaps the Russians might even try to "share the burden" of East Germany's forthcoming leadership transition from Ulbricht—whose heir has not been officially designated.

In evaluating these "optimistic" factors in Soviet motivations, one confronts the following dilemma: Assume for purposes of argument, however

---

*According to Article 13 of the North Atlantic Treaty, "After the Treaty has been in force for twenty years, any Party may cease to be a Party one year after its notice of denunciation has been given . . . ."

unlikely it may be in fact, that a decision (for any or all of the above reasons) has been taken by the Kremlin to seek a fair and equitable settlement of the major East-West security issues. Looking at such a hypothetical decision from the Soviet point of view, it is hard to imagine that the proposed European security conference would be the most desirable vehicle to carry it out. It would be more reasonable and more consistent with past Soviet diplomatic behavior to expect that the Russians would seek to promote quiet talks, at a suitable high level, with the United States, West Germany, and, perhaps, with Britain and France. A quadripartite forum already exists in the Berlin framework and the usual bilateral diplomatic channels are readily available. By contrast, a large East-West conference seems a poor medium for an exploratory feeling out of bargaining positions on highly sensitive subjects. Moreover, diplomatic exploration is alien to the Communist concept of conferences.

Must one then rule out any possibility that desires for a genuine settlement (that is, one which the West could accept) exist in the Soviet system? Westerners who have held private discussions with leading Soviet officials and knowledgeable citizens do not by any means rule out the possibility—although they suggest that the Russians and satellite leaders who favor such a policy are a fragmented minority. Thus, an argument can be made that this minority has seized on a basically propagandistic proposal, made by the controlling faction, and is using it for genuine purposes; therefore, a security conference should be encouraged.

A widely-held view, at least among nonexperts in "Kremlinology," is that it is doubtful that anyone in the West knows enough to predict accurately the inner dynamics of the East.* Making major policy or tactical decisions in the hope of influencing internal Soviet or Warsaw Pact alignments therefore becomes too much a game of blindman's buff.

This is not to say, however, that the West can afford to ignore the genuine forces at work in the East that might one day lead to an end of the division of Europe. Even though a soft line from the West may not strengthen the hand of whatever soft-liners there may be in Eastern Europe, it is possible that an unnecessarily hard line by the West would weaken their case or strengthen

---

*This view is reinforced by some off-the-record comments of a noted scholar and political leader from Czechoslovakia made in the spring of 1968. He replied to a suggestion that the Dubcek "experiment" meant walking a dangerous tightrope: "That is true; but Dubcek will not fall. He alone knows the Russians better than they do themselves—for he grew up there when his parents joined the Czech brigade after the revolution—and he knows what the Soviets are capable of; for almost all of that brigade has been liquidated. So he will make no mistakes in dealing with them." (Six months later, after the massive invasion, Dubcek was taken to Moscow in handcuffs, and he was subsequently deposed by the new Czech leadership.)

their opposition. And there is always the prospect that increased contacts, in and of themselves, could accelerate the mellowing process that is assumed by the West's doctrine of defense cum detente.

There is a third area of possible Soviet motivations to be explored, namely, that within the international Communist movement and between the Soviet Union and its Eastern European allies. In East Germany, Ulbricht's firm opposition to relaxation of tensions is well known. The Rumanians and other advocates of a more open policy toward the West appear to have had considerable success in drafting the Bucharest declaration of 1966. (See Appendix C.) The Rumanians, however, did not even attend the Communist Party meeting at Karlovy Vary. The next phase was the Budapest message addressed by the Warsaw Pact to "all European countries." Coming some seven months after the Soviet invasion of Czechoslovakia and only a month before NATO's twentieth anniversary meeting in Washington, the Budapest appeal for an East-West European security conference was quite apparently an effort to sweep the onus for Czechoslovakia under the rug of detente politics. As one perceptive observer put it,

> A close reading of the Budapest appeal suggested a hard-fought compromise; the Soviets got their appeal . . . the East German and Polish "Hawks" got the pre-conditions on which they had been insisting; and the Czech and Hungarian "Doves" managed to delete most of the traditional polemics.[4]

One can speculate, then, that the Warsaw Pact's proposal for a European security conference may represent a kind of lowest common denominator in intra-Communist politics, the glue by which all can adhere to a common theme—albeit for widely varing reasons. This interpretation is borne out by the fact that numbers of East European political leaders and scholars have expressed support of the idea to dozens of their Western counterparts, and each stresses the beauties of the concept that attract the eye of the particular beholder. More recently, however, according to various dispatches from Eastern Europe, there are some signs that the glue may be dissolving.[5]

Finally, the Soviets clearly have something to be gained by making a good record of peace overtures on the one hand, and demands for a "final solution" to the German problem along orthodox Communist lines on the other, for the benefit of the next major international meeting of the Party.

The precise mix of all of the foregoing elements—and there are undoubtedly others as well—still has the character of the mystery-enigma-riddle that has puzzled Western observers over many decades. For example, Soviet actions with respect to NATO's twentieth anniversary were quite inconsistent with the encouraging tone of the Budapest appeal put forward only a month previously. The Soviets made a point of conducting the largest

naval maneuvers ever held in the Atlantic and Mediterranean areas, and they
issued an official government statement, on the very eve of the meeting, that
appeared to empty their files of all the vituperation accumulated during
twenty years of the cold war.
   In the words of one participant in the NATO session,

> The Soviet statement fell like a great stone into the Ministerial Meeting
> . . . . I watched the AFP ticker item hit the other delegations, as it passed
> from minister to minister with whispers of shock and disbelief. I could
> almost feel the temperature drop in the big air-conditioned State
> Department conference room. "Why," I asked myself for the hun-
> dredth time since the Second World War, "do the Soviets so often slap
> the West across the face with a dead fish just when peace-seeking
> publics have brought governments to the point of doing something that
> might bring negotiations nearer and push war farther away?"[6]

As much as anything, the Soviet statement silenced those NATO Ministers
who wanted to respond to the Budapest appeal; therefore the substance of
the appeal was not mentioned at all in NATO's twentieth anniversary
communique. One cannot help but speculate that this result might have been
intended and that at least some elements of Soviet leadership were afraid that
their offer might be accepted.

Timing and Soviet Tactics

Closely related to questions of tactics and motivations is the question of
timing. The Budapest message states that there are "no compelling reasons
whatever to postpone the convocation of an all-European conference."
Subsequent announcements, both official and unofficial, referred to a
conference in the first half of 1970. One can only speculate about the reasons
behind this apparent urgency. Some connection with SALT? With West
German diplomatic initiatives? Based on an assessment of detente politics and
vulnerability in the West? An anticipated escalation or de-escalation of Soviet
political warfare with Communist China? Tied to a tentative schedule of
important Communist meetings? Or merely standard tactics, like Khrushchev's recurrent deadlines on Berlin?
   The most recent indication of timing, however, was contained in an
unusual statement by the Soviet press spokesman early in January 1970.* He
implied that there had been "slippage" in the original schedule, and that the
conference could be held in the latter half of 1970.[7] Perhaps this slippage

---

*This was also the occasion for an amusing pot-and-kettle exchange between the
Soviet spokesman and a Communist Chinese correspondent. The latter criticized a Soviet
news story and insisted that the press in the U.S.S.R. represented the Soviet government.
The Russian denied this saying that the U.S.S.R. had a free press, to which the Chinese
rejoined mockingly, "A free press—the *Soviet* press?"

reflects a re-evaluation of Western vulnerability to detente overtures, in light of the rather firm line taken at NATO's Ministerial Meeting in December 1969. (See Appendix B.) The latest pronouncements have also begun to refer again to the notion of a "congress of European peoples," an idea which has appeared from time to time, as in the Karlovy Vary conference and in the so-called basic document adopted by the Moscow Conference of Communist and Workers' Parties held in the summer of 1969. Such a congress—in contrast to a conference of governmental representatives—would bring sympathetic West Europeans in contact with Communist ideas and bypass the formal coolness displayed by most Western governments. The Soviet interest in a European trade union congress appears to have similar motivations.

This shift in timing would be interpreted either as a softening-up effort in preparation for a new assault on governments through their public opinion or as an indication of the greater relevance which internal aspects have now come to have—perhaps in relation to a possible future shake-up in the Soviet leadership. Also, of course, a peoples' congress would have a more sympathetic and controllable audience—with less risk that internal disputes would be exploited—than an official conference, where Western nations would be represented by government delegations instead of by selected individuals and organizations.

East European Motivations

The East European countries clearly have differing motivations from those of the Soviet Union. They also differ among themselves, and Russia finds itself attempting to straddle the positions ranging from the hard line of Ulbricht in East Germany and, to a lesser extent, Gomulka in Poland to the "liberal" position of Rumania's Ceausescu and, formerly, Czechoslovakia's Dubcek. The East German (and Polish) conditions for European security include

> the inviolability of existing frontiers in Europe, in particular the frontiers along the Oder-Neisse and the frontier between the Federal Republic of Germany and the German Democratic Republic; international legal recognition of the German Democratic Republic; preventing West Germany from securing atomic weapons in any form, renunciation of the FRG claim to represent all of Germany; the invalidation from the outset of the Munich Agreement of 1939, and the banning of neo-Nazi organizations.[8]

Czechoslovakia is the only Warsaw Pact member except East Germany to have a Western frontier, that is, a border shared with a nation of West Europe. It is concerned with the German problem; yet the Czechs are still recovering from the trauma of the Warsaw Pact invasion, the Soviet occupation, and the ensuing political shake-up. The nations of the so-called Southern Tier of the

Pact—Hungary, Rumania, and Bulgaria—are somewhat less preoccupied with the German question: Rumania in particular has played the role of a France in the East, demonstrating a rather maverick foreign policy line, in intriguing contrast to the strictly orthodox Communism pursued at home.

It is apparent that the more liberal of the East European countries welcome an East-West European security conference as a device for increasing their freedom of maneuver vis-à-vis the Soviet Union. And such maneuvering room and flexibility is presumably in the long-range interests of the West. By the same token, it can be argued that the conference must be regarded by the Soviets as a two-edged sword. To be sure, one edge of the blade can cut at support of NATO in Western public opinion, promote the de facto ratification of the status quo in Germany without the necessity for concessions, and help bury the unpleasant image of Czechoslovakia. But the other edge of the blade can be used to cut into Soviet control over the East European desire to play at "Westpolitik," to expose to public view the differences within the Pact, and perhaps even to set in motion liberalizing tendencies within the East. While the Soviet occupation of Czechoslovakia remains as a stern reminder that there are limits to "Westpolitik" and to liberalization, an open conference does make it harder to spank one's children in public, so to speak.

Some observers feel that a new East-West conference on European security would really be of very doubtful net interest to the Soviet Union, that is, if one were actually held. Therefore, it might turn out to be like the slogan of "general and complete disarmament," with which Communist propaganda machines had a field day for almost a decade, until this theme was also adopted as a goal by the United States. Since then, little has been heard of "GCD," and there has in fact been progress on practical and concrete arms control measures. But the combination of inherent limits and constraints on the East Europeans, plus the applicability of the earlier observation that the West cannot really play the inner dynamics of the East, would seem to cast doubts over the desirability of a conference for these reasons.

Tests of Sincerity

Given all these uncertainties of tactics and motivations, can tests of sincerity be devised which would be reliable guideposts for the West in deciding on its own tactics and procedures for a possible conference? As noted earlier, Secretary of State Rogers suggested three such tests at the NATO Ministerial Meeting in December 1969. These were, quadripartite negotiations about Berlin, Eastern responses to the German diplomatic initiatives, and mutual force reductions. Although the earlier discussion of these substantive issues makes it doubtful that much progress can be found as evidence of passing these tests of sincerity, it may also be too soon to say that the East has "failed" them. On the other hand, the Prague agenda, put forward by the Warsaw Pact in October 1969 for the European security conference, does not specifically mention any of the three. (See Appendix C.) It proposes instead declarations on the non-use of force and an expansion of East-West trade. It remains to be seen whether this suggested agenda (described as open ended in the Prague communique) is merely a negotiating position and is really regarded as flexible by the East.

The Soviets are improving their performance, however, on one other possible test of realism in approaching the problem, namely the question of participation. The initial formulation stressed that the conference should be "all-European," including, of course, the Russians but excluding the United States and Canada. This was a pretty clear propaganda reflection of the long-standing effort to depict the United States as a "foreign" influence in Europe and to undercut the Atlantic symbol. It tended to reveal the non-serious nature of the proposal, since the Soviets know as well as anyone else that North American participation is a sine qua non for substantive progress on European security matters.

Following the Budapest declaration, however, the message began to be spread, in innumerable East-West contacts, that there was no real objection to American participation. And the official Soviet formulation at the January 13, 1970, press conference included American and Canadian participation from the outset.* It is a moot question whether the Soviet Union's change of heart can be interpreted as an increase in realism or whether it merely reflects an assessment that—in view of NATO's clear-cut position, maintained for many months, that the United States and Canada must participate from the outset—the Allies could not be divided on this issue.

Still another test of sincerity, and perhaps the major one, will be the resumption of SALT at Vienna in April 1970. Although European security as such will not be discussed, it may be possible to deduce from the progress (or lack of it) at the talks whether the Soviets seem determined to press for some form of superiority in strategic weapons. If so, this hardly bodes well for a reduction of tensions in the major area of conflict between American and Russian interests. But if some dialogue leading to an understanding, if not an

---

*Although the Soviet claim to be a European power, in contrast to the United States, has some historical and geographic weight, the United States is, in fact, more closely linked by culture and tradition to Western Europe and is closer to it in the jet age than most of Russia. It might be interesting, however, to propose a conference from which both the United States and Russia would be excluded. The United States would certainly be less nervous about what its allies would be saying at such a convocation than Russia would be about the conduct of its satellites; and the resulting tensions within the socialist camp might be interesting to observe.

agreement, can be reached, then this will be the clearest available evidence that the forces working for a longer-term settlement of the overall East-West division in Europe may be in the ascendency.

Procedural Aspects

Finally, there is the question of procedures for such a conference.[9] It is worth noting here that diplomatic history seems to reveal two lessons about conference diplomacy: there is a direct ratio between the extent of prior preparations and the probability of success of a conference; and there is an inverse relationship between the number of participants and the outcome of the conference. One specific proposal for a European security conference was the Finnish initiative of May 5, 1969. Letters were sent to all European governments and to the United States and Canada, calling for a meeting at Helsinki early in 1970. The details, however, were not spelled out, pending reactions to the proposal.[10] As any experienced conference observer knows, the details, including the size and shape of the tables, are of the essence, especially in cases where some of the participants do not formally recognize each other.

Without an agreed agenda—and a common interpretation of what is to be discussed—an international conference usually involves little more than speech-making, at best, and an exchange of polemics, at worst. No government—Washington, Moscow, or any other—is prepared to have decisions on its vital interests taken on an ad hoc basis by the caucus of a delegation attending a conference, no matter how high-ranking its members or how swift its telecommunications back to its capital. The preparatory phase must therefore include enough advance information about the proposals likely to be made by the other side to permit each party to process its positions through its own internal political machinery.

This very point suggests one conceivable purpose of a conference on European security which has not yet been mentioned. This would be to have an East-West meeting whose agenda was exclusively devoted to procedures for exploring solutions to the problems of European security. That is, the conference might merely ratify existing bilateral or multilateral talks, giving a stamp of approval to SALT, to inter-German bilateral discussions, to four-power negotiations about the future of Berlin, to activities of the so-called Group of Ten, and to any relationships that may exist between European security and the work in progress at the Eighteen Nation Disarmament Conference in Geneva. But such a nonsubstantive conference has few major advantages and has the disadvantage of dealing only in appearances.

If it appeared that some additional forum were desirable, then the procedual conference could presumably propose the establishment of some ongoing institutional machinery or organizational vehicle, such as the commission on European security that has been proposed in a previous study[11] and informally suggested by the British. But rather than have the commission initiate proposals on substantive issues for consideration by governments, it might make more sense for the commission to receive, analyze, and test the acceptability of ideas put forward relatively informally by governments through their representatives on the commission. Thus, it might perform a useful catalytic and consensus-building function by defining any areas in which progress seems possible, without forcing governments to commit themselves in advance or confronting them with the prospect of receiving unacceptable recommendations or badly split reports from the commission.

Such a continuing commission—indeed it might equally well be called an institute—could deal also with matters of East-West economic analysis and trade, possibly also with cultural and scientific affairs (including problems of the global environment), and with ideas on security issues such as mutual force reductions. Force reductions, however, would not really seem to need the establishment of a commission, unless a long-term educational process were envisaged, since procedures for NATO-Warsaw Pact or government-to-government discussions of a specific proposal could be worked out at a procedural conference itself. And as noted earlier, the economic, cultural, and scientific aspects have inherent limits and are already being dealt with through bilateral or multilateral channels.

One other element of "conferencemanship" needs to be considered, namely, the role of the press. It was widely held to be a good omen for SALT that both sides agreed that there would be no substantive briefings of the press. Normal conference practice is for each side to brief the members of its own press corps in attendance, both before and after important sessions. This, of course, is countered by similar tactics by other delegations, with the net result often being confusion, rather than clarity. The problem of press briefings is a major one even in NATO, whose internal differences are minor in comparison with those to be expected in an East-West meeting which could easily fall victim to the tendency of one of the delegations to make propaganda, whether or not that was their original aim. On the other hand, an active role for the press does give the East European countries a chance to make known their own views, independent of the Soviet Union—which is an advantage to be balanced against the disadvantages of propaganda dissemination.

Finally, any conference also involves the very real dangers of false expectations. The West might well be concerned that unfounded hopes of an imminent breakthrough in East-West relations might undercut public support for the Western defense posture which has to be maintained until an East-West settlement is a reality. It is also possible that disappointment in the outcome of a conference might jeopardize the chances of pursuing satisfactory substantive East-West accords through more useful channels. In short, a highly publicized, unstructured, international conference has a tendency to develop a circus atmosphere; and this is as likely to retard as to achieve real progress.

6 Detente in the 1970's

A hard look at the actors and their motivations, and the issues and their history, makes it difficult to avoid a negative short-run conclusion about the Soviet call for a new East-West conference on European security. For it is, in Shakespeare's terms, but a play within the play; and as currently proposed, the conference would have very little to do with European security—at least as the West would define it.

Neither the German problem and Berlin nor mutual force reductions nor other security questions high on the West's priority agenda is included in the East's proposed agenda. The first item called for by the East, renunciations of force, would have meaning only if the Soviet Union in effect disavowed its rights of intervention under the enemy-states articles of the United Nations Charter and reversed the Brezhnev Doctrine of limited sovereignty within the socialist commonwealth. The former might conceivably be abandoned in exchange for West German renunciations, but it is hard to see how the problem of the Brezhnev Doctrine could be dealt with. The Western nations specifically rejected it in the wake of Czechoslovakia, and they could hardly accept it now by the indirect route of renouncing force while overlooking the only recent case where force has been used in Europe. Nor would the Soviets be likely to retract formally the doctrine by which that use of force was rationalized.

The other conference agenda item proposed by the East is expansion of trade. It hardly requires a security conference to endorse what the prevailing political and economic conditions permit or require in terms of East-West trade, although there are political advantages for the West in maximizing contacts with the East and an argument can be made that the conference "atmospherics" might be helpful.

Furthermore, the evidence available about Soviet motivations in proposing the conference is not encouraging. It seems all too clear that the Russian purposes are primarily propagandistic—for example, to depict the American and German role in Europe as the cause of continuing tension, to exploit Western desires for detente, and to blur remembrance of the invasion of Czechoslovakia. It is also seen as a means to achieve standard Soviet and East German political objectives: recognition of the German Democratic Republic and ratification of the status quo without any concessions, for example, on Berlin. And finally, there are some indications that the proposal is as much directed at the internal politics of the Communist movement as at external considerations. It is this last aspect which gives rise to some of the reasons advanced in the West for agreeing to hold such a conference. But the assumption that the East Europeans—and perhaps the soft-line factions within the Soviet hierarchy—would gain in real influence thereby seems tenuous. The freedom to maneuver which they hope to obtain could be short lived, for the argument that trends toward independence in Eastern Europe are irreversible in a detente climate has been answered all too clearly in Prague.

One reaches a different answer, however, to the question "Are there significant Western interests in resolving European security issues?" The argument that time is working against the Communist ability to maintain the status quo indefinitely is offset by a growing impatience within Western public opinion at the costs—political and economic—of maintaining it. Some of this European impatience is reflected in the Federal Republic's *Ostpolitik* and in the popularity of detente politics among the left wing of European political parties, coalitions, and governments. Indeed, in Belgium, Italy, and occasionally in Britain, accord on this approach to foreign policy is the cement which has held together otherwise incompatible political factions. And in the United States support for it can readily be found on Capitol Hill.

However one evaluates the prospects for the success of *Ostpolitik*—with the East or in terms of West German politics—it seems clear that the West ought not to ratify the status quo with regard to either diplomatic recognition of East Germany or the German boundary question, unless a more viable solution to the problem of Berlin can be found and a framework of inter-German relationships provided which is both stable and adaptable to the context of a wider and longer-term East-West accommodation. But there should be no expectations that the irreconcilable conflict between East and West over the medium-term future of the two Germanies can be papered over. Important steps are within the limits of possibility and could be taken if the East is willing to make matching concessions. But a security conference seems an unlikely forum in which to seek the evidence of such willingness.

The interests of both sides, as outlined earlier, could also be served by a realistic approach to mutual force reductions. But again, there is no evidence to date of any interest from the other side in pursuing this objective in a security conference setting.

Thus, when one holds the conference-proposal jewel up to the light and examines each of its facets, it must be branded paste; the real diamond—and issues of European security are as hard as diamond—has not been offered. The paste gem, nevertheless, has a certain glitter and attractiveness, growing out of a genuine Western desire to make progress in East-West relations. It is possible that the West may not need to deal with the specific proposals already advanced, for there are signs of flagging Soviet interest in convening a conference or congress in the immediate future. But the conference idea may—and probably will—arise again, and in any case, the issues of European security remain to be dealt with in the context of the longer-term trends of international politics.

Dilemmas for the East

As the decade of the 1970's opens, the Russians and East Europeans find themselves in a series of powerful dilemmas. On the one hand, they are both fascinated and repelled by *Ostpolitik;* desires for West German trade and credits mingle with genuine fears of revanchism. The pronounced Russian strand in German policy throughout this century and the equally strong German element in Russian diplomacy seem straining to meet each other almost unconsciously. Yet, for the Russians, maintaining a firm hold on East Germany, the industrial heart of COMECON and the military bastion of the Soviet's forward presence in Central and Eastern Europe, retains top priority.

In the long run, the Soviet Union must doubt its ability to keep orthodox and subservient Communist parties in control in Eastern Europe. To permit the Czech internal heresy or the external dissidence of Rumania, would threaten the political-ideological base of the Soviet system itself. Yet, to take steps such as the invastion of Czechoslovakia arouses reactions which further fragment the international Communist movement. Inside Russia a disappointing economic picture, which has many unsolved structural problems, combines with youth unrest and unmet consumer demands, giving pause to confidence in long-term stability. On her eastern flank the Soviet Union perceives a threat from China, a danger exacerbated by an ideological rift which has split the Communist world.

The Soviet dilemma extends to relations with the United States, which is still engaged in an undeclared war with Russia's "socialist ally" in Vietnam but with whom strategic arms limitation talks have both economic and military logic. Russia's traditional sensitivity to containment—as practiced by the British in the nineteenth century, by Allied forces during the Russian civil war, by "capitalist-fascist encirclers" in the 1930's, and by American governments since World War II—seems to have been intensified by the resumption of American-Chinese talks, to a degree quite out of proportion to the significance of the talks. The Soviets must hope that the United States will disengage from Europe and go home, as they have so often urged it to do, yet they also fear this move, which would deprive Russia of a constant in the formula for European security.

In summary, the Russian horoscope shows trouble at home, trouble in dealing with Eastern Europe, trouble in the triangular relationship with the American capitalist enemy and the Chinese Communist opponent in the international Communist movement, and last, though not least, trouble in coping with the resurgence of Western Europe and West Germany. With all the ills that Western societies and diplomacy may be heir to, it is hard to conceive of a Western leader who would want to exchange his headaches for the Russian portfolio of problems.

Options for the West

This then is the challenge that confronts the West in dealing with the Soviet Union in a time of change and turmoil. There is little that the West can do to influence overtly the *internal* politics of the Communist world—although known stresses can be affected by American actions, say, in Vietnam. Even if their dynamics were understood sufficiently, diplomatic intervention might well prove counterproductive: too much encouragement of East European independence and "Westpolitik" could bring another Czechoslovakia; too close a rapprochement with China could end SALT. Yet too relaxed a Western policy—and *détente* means "relaxation" in French—could encourage American disengagement, unilateral force reductions, and a gradual crumbling of the defense pillar of Western diplomacy. One cannot predict flatly that such developments would not be matched on the Eastern side; but the internal politics, imperatives, and controls of the Communist system argue against it.

In the end, the critical questions about approaches to European security boil down to this: Does the East or the West stand to gain more from a relaxation of tensions? And the answer is that the West gains more from the reality of detente, whereas the East gains more from its mere appearances. For the reality would have to extend to the East, and it would be inconsistent with the type of political control maintained by Russia over the East European countries through their Communist parties and with the forms of domination maintained by those parties over the peoples concerned. So the tactical problem for the West is how to insure that the realities accompany appearances—or that appearances do not outrun realities.

One theoretical way to meet this tactical problem would be to mount such a powerful political-military posture that the costs of matching it might lead the East to sue for a realistic "peace"; but in practice, the result would probably be just the contrary. At the other extreme, the West could so disarm itself unilaterally that not even the most extreme paranoid in the East could find a "capitalist threat"—and then the Communists might relax. But given their preconceptions and the strong factions opposing any relaxation, they might instead merely find opportunities to consummate the ideological conquest which lack of openings has increasingly relegated to the level of rhetoric.

Discounting these extremes, the West could seek to adopt a defensive stand: puncturing false appearances by resisting conference overtures; insisting on substantive negotiations of the major East-West issues; minimizing contacts with the East; and withholding trade, credit, and technology in the hope that some "realities" might then be lured forth from the East. Alternatively, the West could take up the lead given by Willy Brandt and challenge the East with attractive political and economic opportunities, hoping that the ensuing momentum of detente would be irresistible.

Of these two middle options, the first, or defensive, approach has two defects: it is not in keeping with the present mood of politics in the Atlantic world and would be difficult to maintain; and by discouraging the forces in the East who favor movement toward accomodation; it might miss real opportunities for progress in East-West relations. The second alternative also has two defects. For one thing, there are clear limits to how far the East can go in adjusting the status quo; given those inherent brakes, the West might merely build up false appearances in its own constituencies and increase, rather than reduce, the asymmetrical effects of detente in East and West by, as President Nixon put it, becoming "psychologically dependent" on extravagant expectations. The other defect is illustrated by a Frenchman's description of the detente process: "seducing the East until she gets a little bit pregnant." Unfortunately, as Czechoslovakia has shown, the Soviet abortion knife is always at the ready.

Before plotting a course which tries to avoid these defects, it is well to ask what the West really wants to happen in the East. Most people would agree with British Foreign Minister Stewart that "we must, unless we are to despair of mankind, approach with hope the concept of trying to get easier relations between . . . the Communist and the non-Communist worlds."[1] Given a choice, the West would probably choose to avert, rather than encourage, a realization of the cataclysmic prediction by a Soviet author that before 1980 there will be a Soviet war with China, possibly with some nuclear weapons used; large-scale and bloody uprisings in Russia; and a breakup of the Soviet empire.[2] For such a cataclysm might well be catalytic—in the sense of starting a chain reaction of international violence which could engulf the world. And even if that risk were to be discounted, America and its allies have passed the point of believing that the self-immolation of their ideological enemies would solve their own problems.

Rather, an awareness is growing that all of today's ideologies and their shibboleths may be irrelevant to the staggering problems of the mass societies of tomorrow. The end of Soviet rule in Russia might, to be sure, open the way to substantial savings in military spending, but this would contribute nothing at all to the West's understanding of how to use those resources effectively in tackling its internal problems.

So the long-range hope must be that the Russians—and the Chinese too—will sooner or later come to this same type of perception about the essential irrelevance to their own vital interests of their international enmities and tabescent ideologies. Such an awareness, coupled with recognition that the West is not really interested in the destruction of the East's systems, can bring about the much-needed "pragmatic revolution" in world affairs. That revolution would involve putting the world's best minds, wherever located, to work in developing the economic, social, political, technological, biogenetic, and ecological tools to insure a livable world in the next millennium. Its beginning—and the doubling of population expected to accompany it—lies a bare thirty years in the future. So the "long term"—in which global cooperation may be compulsory instead of capricious—is not as far away as it used to be.

Even if one regards this forecast as visionary, there is not much doubt that ultimately this is the direction in which the world must move, for even a "durable peace" cannot be an end in itself; it may merely be the minimum prerequisite to human survival. In the short term therefore, the West should seek modes of relationships with the East which encourage cooperative pragmatism. But it is hard to quarrel with President Nixon's judgment that a change in Communist purposes will not be advanced by underestimating the depth of disparity or fostering illusions about negotiations.[3]

Given its own dilemmas—including the conflict on the left with Rumania and on the "right" with East Germany—Soviet policy toward the West will be a mixture of threats and promises, detente and hostility, and cooperation and competition which will not always be internally consistent at any given time. And it makes sense for Western policy to be flexible in choosing among the various elements of its options regarding European security.

But the two key elements—realism and initiatives—must be clear enough to mislead neither Western publics nor Eastern policy makers. The West needs to clarify its thinking on the essentiality of a stable political balance in Europe, on the military underpinnings of that balance, and on the division of labor in maintaining it. Having done so, it can take the initiative of putting forward a simple, realistic, and phased proposal for mutual force reductions in Europe. Each stage should become a floor on troop strengths, as well as a ceiling, until carried out by both sides, thus assuring the continuity of stability. Given the central importance of strategic arms, the United States should then proceed, in close consultation with NATO, to probe Soviet attitudes in SALT, avoiding any openings which would allow the Soviets to divide America from its allies.[4]

With respect to the crucial problems of Germany and Berlin, realism is essential. The West German *Ostpolitik* constitutes a valuable component of the forward arm of Western diplomacy, and it deserves full backing from West Germany's allies. At the same time, these allies—especially the three whose status in Berlin guards the city's viability—have special interests in working out a less dangerous version of the present situation, if not, indeed, a long-term Berlin solution. In addition to meeting this interest, the basic status quo between West and East Germany needs to be surrounded with whatever aura of all-German relationships is necessary for political acceptability—and hence stability. These two points should be the minimum Western conditions for the "normalization" which the East Europeans seek in terms of recognition for East Germany and boundary settlements.

Renunciation of force, despite its misleading simplicity, does have meaning in the special German context; but while it is perfectly acceptable as a device for improving the atmospherics, the West must avoid the pitfall of implicitly accepting Soviet claims under either the "enemy states" provisions of the United Nations Charter, or the Brezhnev Doctrine regarding Eastern Europe.

Finally, notwithstanding the inherent limitations imposed by the nature of the Communist system and by market factors, the West could well afford to make and publicize an offer of liberalized exchanges with Eastern Europe. These have fluctuated in the past between politicization and functionalism. But today, in the context of the other measures discussed above, these should be packaged and given a political message. The gist of that message might well be as follows:

The Western allies can and will prevent the imposition of the Communist version of a "solution" to the problems of European security; and they will not be deluded by security conference proposals which have little to do with the issues of security. But they have an interest in the stability and long-term development of the "other social and political system," and can pledge themselves not to change it by force or seek to undermine its internal security. They would be willing to cosponsor a conference to ratify such undertakings on a mutual basis and to review the several tracks in which substantive negotiations on security issues are or could be under way.

Moreover, the West is willing to adopt an umbrella policy under which individual states would seek to expand trade, cultural, tourist, and scientific exchanges with countries of the East by a growing percentage each year. Their collective policy in such bodies as the European Common Market, the Organization for Economic Cooperation and Development, COCOM (the Coordinating Committee for Strategic Trade Controls), and the United Nations Economic Commission for Europe will reflect this objective to the extent possible on individual issues and where consistent with improvements in overall East-West security, e.g., Germany, mutual force reductions, and SALT. And finally, they invite the East to join in a dialogue (either in the Economic Commission for Europe or in a special commission or institute set up for the purpose) on those pragmatic technological challenges with environmental dimensions which overshadow ideological and political differences.

The environmental aspect of the Western initiative deserves elaboration. An East-West commission to improve the international dialogue on the increasing challenges of the global environment could be a vehicle for sublimating those detente urges which conflict with realism. All interested countries could be given membership—possibly on a rotating basis—on political or technological subcommittees. Moreover, Berlin would provide a suitable East-West location and give that city a truly international mission. It is just possible that a growing perception by international elites that the world is in fact a "closed ecological system" (and one which an astronaut might describe as having "diminishing life-support capabilities") could in time transform conventional images of the relative importance of traditional issues such as European security. Even if the initial Communist reaction were to be, "Only capitalists pollute," it is hard to see how discussions of this issue and the scientific evidence bearing thereon could be harmful. And a dialogue involving such common purposes might help improve the diplomatic atmosphere for a European settlement.

Whether or not this particular initiative proves practicable,* there is no inherent conflict between the two criteria suggested for Western diplomacy: a

---

*It is worth noting that when President Nixon, shortly after he took office, proposed that NATO study "problems of modern societies," he was almost alone in believing that

conservative realism in substance, and a procedural forward posture of taking the initiative. President Nixon has correctly pointed out that negotiations "are served neither by bluff abroad nor bluster at home." As in domestic politics, however, initiatives—even ones announced publicly—need not be insincere or unrealistic.

Because the Soviets sometimes play the game purely for propaganda stakes, there is no reason for the West to limit its concentration on the issues to a defensive turning aside of tactical ploys from the East. Instead, since it has substantive ideas to put forward, Western diplomacy should take the lead in so doing. And this is where the President's "New Strategy for Peace"[5] is open to criticism. For its concern for realism in negotiations and its opposition to "naive enthusiasm" appears to miss a point which is common to both metaphysics and politics: appearances can influence reality; or, as the lawyers like to say, "substance is secreted in the interstices of procedure."

There is no reason for the West to appear to the East—let alone to its own publics—as immobile, negative, and defensive on European security. If the Soviet proposal for a security conference is devoid of substance, why not respond with a substantive challenge on mutual force reductions or exchanges or an environmental dialogue? And if no substantive agenda can be agreed upon but a conference could provide useful atmospherics, why not propose an essentially procedural conference, either limited to the membership of NATO and the Warsaw Pact or including also certain European neutrals. Here the objectives would be to "ratify" the overall, long-term goal of a stable settlement in Europe and, in effect, to endorse as means the several forums in which substantive issues either are already being discussed—SALT, the Four Powers on Berlin, and the German bilaterals—or could be considered—a NATO-Pact exploration of mutual force reductions and, perhaps, even the Eighteen Nation Disarmament Conference or the so-called East-West Group of Ten. Such a conference might also evolve proposals for new organizational machinery, if a need existed, for example, a continuing commission or institute on problems of East-West relations, perhaps to include ecology and environment.

At best, the several key East-West dialogues would receive a multilateral blessing; and at worst, a rejection of such initiatives by the East would merely reconfirm the obvious—that a final settlement in Europe is a long-term evolutionary process.

---

the idea either would take hold or could be a useful ingredient of the "West-West" political dialogue. But to the surprise of his advisors and critics, it has caught on with vigor in the Atlantic Alliance.

One argument that can be made against a "forward" option is that this might stimulate unrealistic detente politics in Europe and lend support in Washington to the Mansfield Resolution for troop withdrawals. But such substantive initiatives as that proposed here for mutual force reductions can gain interest in and support for maintaining a stable military balance in Europe; and the unconvinced are not likely to be converted by an immobile defense of the status quo in any case. There are, of course, some risks both ways; but the lesser risk—and the greater gain—may be to set realistic limits to the diplomatic objectives, even while pursuing them vigorously. "We must remember," said Manlio Brosio, NATO's Secretary General, "that a policy of initiative towards negotiations seems to be the most effective one for keeping allied solidarity strong. Passivity may foster doubt and frustration."[6]

One other "option" needs to be mentioned briefly—that of "Europeanizing" the problems of European security. For the political and military reasons already set forth, such a "de-Americanization" is not a valid option; but it is an increasingly popular argument nevertheless, despite the fact that the situations in Europe and Vietnam are totally different—not least because America's stake in Europe and the challenge to it are of a greatly different order of magnitude. But the real reason is that the objectives in Europe are stability and long-term progress toward East-West cooperation. And both would be jeopardized by American disengagement in reliance on the faint hope of a European risorgimento, which would be even less of a possibility in the crisis of confidence which an American withdrawal would precipitate.

Assuming, then, that the choices essentially lie in the modalities of approach, it is the conclusion of this study that a policy of initiatives offers less risks of anticipatory relaxation of Western defense efforts and more prospects of eventual East-West progress than the more passive and defensive option.[7] But realism, as opposed to empty posturing, is essential to give to a forward policy credibility in both East and West.

Probably more important than the selection of the precise variants within either option is a public understanding of both the importance and the difficulties of reaching a secure new relationship between East and West in Europe.

A conceivable "package deal" has already been outlined on a piecemeal basis in this book: if the East would yield its heretofore inflexible position on Berlin and agree to give appropriate guarantees for the continued viability of the city, then Bonn, and the West generally, might legally recognize the German Democratic Republic, formalize diplomatic relations (although West Germany might register a reservation for the record on the moral legitimacy of the Eastern regime), and give de jure acceptance to the Polish and Czech frontiers. Following the diplomatic initiative of Chancellor Brandt's *Ost-*

politik and NATO's declared policy for detente, inter-German affairs and overall East-West relations could move toward normalization by agreement to increase trade, travel, cultural, economic, and technological relations by a specified percentage annually. Paralleling or even preceding this progress in the nonmilitary field, a phased program of mutual and balanced force reductions could also be agreed upon, and a multilateral "non-use of force" agreement could serve as the wrapping for the package, assuming that a way could be found around the Brezhnev Doctrine impediment.

Such a package deal would involve some significant concessions by East and West. For the West, these consist mostly of applying the de jure label to a twenty-five-year de facto coexistence with the status quo. The East's concessions would be on Berlin, on liberalizing contacts, and, ideologically, on implicitly abandoning a claim to change the status quo in the West.

The point of listing these elements of a potential bargain is not to suggest that an agreement of such scope is a near-term possibility; for the several individual elements would each have to be explored and negotiated, and as previously explained, each element is quite complicated in its own right. The point is, rather, to illustrate that even the most optimistic package which lies within the range of the possible for the early 1970's would not, by itself, solve Europe's problems—let alone the world's.

The dilemmas for the East, noted earlier, would remain, and perhaps they would even be sharpened by this degree of reality in detente. Pressures of various kinds on the West might be somewhat reduced, but a substantial NATO and American defense posture in Europe would still be needed to keep the bargain honest. Fundamental ideological antagonism between East and West—and within the East—would be likely to persist. And the basic status quo thus sanctified might well prove to have a short half-life—compared, say, with that of the Congress of Vienna—as technology, generational perceptions, and population growth continue their explosive rate of change.

Given these considerations, a new East-West conference on European security hardly seems likely to produce a "grand settlement" of the main issues which divide Europe in 1970.

But parallel progress on bilateral and multilateral negotiating tracks, perhaps followed by a series of exploratory meetings and continuing East-West consultation in various forums, might move toward amelioration of the central questions of European security and the underlying political conflict. The forward policy of initiatives recommended in this book might at least make a beginning. And the aim of that beginning would be not too much different from the aim of today's policies: an East-West political equilibrium which rests on a stable military balance. This continental balance, like its international counterpart between the superpowers, can be maintained at lower levels of economic cost, of tension, and of risk. This end, while modest, might in turn be the beginning of progress toward the more noble goal of a truly cooperative international system based on East-West harmony. This, then, is a worthy agenda for the detente diplomacy which concerns the United States and European security during the 1970's.

Appendixes

A

The Military Balance between NATO and the Warsaw Pact

The Military Balance between NATO and the Warsaw Pact

(Excluding consideration of strategic weapons and seapower.)

Any assessment of the balance between NATO and the Warsaw Pact involves both comparison of the strengths of men and equipment, including nuclear weapons, and consideration of qualitative characteristics such as geographical advantages, deployment, training and logistic support. Inevitably there are difficulties in giving values to qualitative factors and in deciding on their relevance. The comparisons which follow are therefore primarily a quantitative guide to the balance and necessarily oversimplify what is by its nature a complex problem.

Ground Forces

The ground forces in the alliance systems are deployed in Northern, Central and Southern Europe. There are, however, difficulties in making precise calculations about this distribution since it might, for example, depend on circumstances whether Soviet formations in Western Russia would be committed to the Baltic area or to Germany. For such reasons Northern and Central Europe are grouped together in the tables which follow and Southern Europe is shown separately.

Ground Formations

Category	Northern and Central Europe[a]			Southern Europe[b]		
	NATO	Warsaw Pact	(of which USSR)	NATO	Warsaw Pact	(of which USSR)
Ground forces available to commanders in peace-time (in division equivalents)						
—armoured	8	30	*19*	6	11	*3*
—infantry, mechanized and airborne	16	35	*20*	27	23	*4*

Notes *a* and *b* will be found at the end of Appendix A.

If French formations are included with NATO, Western forces available in peace-time would be increased by 5 mechanized divisions.

These comparisons do not, however, reflect an accurate quantitative assessment, since NATO formations are much larger than those of the Warsaw Pact. . . . . It is necessary to take account not only of this difference in size,

Reprinted, with permission, from the Appendix to *The Military Balance, 1969-1970* (London: The Institute for Strategic Studies, 1969), pages 62-63.

but also of the other combat troops in formations higher than brigades, and of those men who directly support them. Figures calculated on this basis—and the calculation can only be approximate—give the following comparison for forces in peace-time:

Manpower (in thousands)

	Northern and Central Europe[a]			Southern Europe[b]		
Category	NATO	Warsaw Pact	(of which USSR)	NATO	Warsaw Pact	(of which USSR)
Combat and direct support troops available	600	925	*600*	525	375	*100*

Notes *a* and *b* will be found at the end of Appendix A.

If French forces were included the Western figure for Northern and Central Europe might be increased by some 100,000.

The mobilization of first line reserves and the movement of other reinforcements by both sides would materially alter the above balance during the initial stages of mobilization, when the Warsaw Pact countries would have a superior reinforcement capacity derived in part from their geographical situation. There is also the possibility that the Warsaw Pact might begin to mobilize before NATO did. If, however, a European crisis developed gradually enough to permit full reinforcement, the West would be in a position much more resembling equality, since the NATO countries in fact maintain larger armies than the Warsaw Pact. The figures are for Army/Marines (in thousands) for NATO 3,550 and the Warsaw Pact countries 2,847. If French forces are included, the Western figure becomes 3,878. Of course large numbers of these men are outside Europe, as for example American forces in Asia and Soviet forces on their Far Eastern frontier.

Tanks

The relative tank strengths are as follows:

	Northern and Central Europe[a]			Southern Europe[b]		
Category	NATO	Warsaw Pact	(of which USSR)	NATO	Warsaw Pact	(of which USSR)
Medium/heavy tanks available to commanders —in peace-time	5,250	12,500	*8,000*	1,800	4,600	*1,300*

Notes *a* and *b* will be found at the end of Appendix A.

It will be seen that NATO has rather less than half as many tanks as the Warsaw Pact in Northern and Central Europe, though the NATO tanks are generally more modern and their armament is probably better. Bearing in mind the essentially defensive role of NATO the deficiency may be less significant than the figures suggest, particularly as NATO has some 50 per cent superiority over the Warsaw Pact in anti-tank weapons. Conventional artillery is not shown in the table but both sides are about equal in strength: NATO is, however, likely to have superior fire-power because of the greater accuracy of its weapons and the greater lethality of its ammunition, and the logistic capability to sustain higher rates of fire.

Air Forces

The aircraft strengths in peace-time are as follows:

Category	Northern and Central Europe[a]			Southern Europe[b]		
	NATO	Warsaw Pact	(of which USSR)	NATO	Warsaw Pact	(of which USSR)
Tactical aircraft in operational service						
–light bombers	50	260	*220*	–	60	*60*
–fighter/ground attack	1,150	1,285	*820*	550	215	*105*
–interceptors	450	2,000	*885*	300	860	*295*
–reconnaissance	400	250	*220*	125	50	*40*

Notes *a* and *b* will be found at the end of Appendix A.

The division of tactical aircraft into the categories shown can only be a very approximate one since some aircraft can be adapted to more than one kind of mission. In general NATO has a higher proportion of multipurpose aircraft and NATO aircraft have a greater average capability: they have longer range and over twice the average payload on typical missions. NATO crews get about twice as many flying hours a month on training as their Warsaw Pact counterparts. It is difficult to determine the extent to which the greater performance and versatility of the NATO aircraft would offset the greater numbers of the Warsaw Pact, though it is evident enough that a direct comparison of the two air forces in terms solely of numbers may be misleading, and could undervalue NATO's real capability. But it could be equally misleading to give weight to these qualitative factors without taking into account the different compositions of the two air forces, and the different roles they would be called upon to play in war, conventional or nuclear.

There is one other factor. The East enjoys a numerical superiority in Europe but the NATO inventory of aircraft world-wide is far greater than that of the Warsaw Pact. NATO therefore has a greater reinforcement capability.

Notes to Appendix A

[a]Includes, on the NATO side, the commands for which AFCENT and AFNORTH commanders have responsibility (see introduction to NATO section). France is not included. On the Warsaw Pact side it includes the command for which the Pact High Commander has responsibility, but excludes the armed forces of Bulgaria, Hungary and Rumania. Soviet units normally stationed in the Western USSR and such troops as might be committed to the Baltic theatre of operations have, however, been included on the Warsaw Pact side.

[b]Includes, on the NATO side, the Italian, Greek, and Turkish land forces and such American and British units as would be committed to the Mediterranean theatre of operations, and on the Warsaw Pact side, the land forces of Bulgaria, Hungary and Rumania, and such Soviet units normally stationed in Hungary and Southern USSR as might be committed to the Mediterranean theatre.

B   NATO Documents

The Future Tasks of the Alliance

(Harmel Report to the North Atlantic Council)

1. A year ago, on the initiative of the Foreign Minister of Belgium, the governments of the fifteen nations of the Alliance resolved to "study the future tasks which face the Alliance, and its procedures for fulfilling them in order to strengthen the Alliance as a factor for durable peace". The present report sets forth the general tenor and main principles emerging from this examination of the future tasks of the Alliance.

2. Studies were undertaken by Messrs. Schütz, Watson, Spaak, Kohler and Patijn. The Council wishes to express its appreciation and thanks to these eminent personalities for their efforts and for the analyses they produced.

3. The exercise has shown that the Alliance is a dynamic and vigorous organization which is constantly adapting itself to changing conditions. It also has shown that its future tasks can be handled within the terms of the Treaty by building on the methods and procedures which have proved their value over many years.

4. Since the North Atlantic Treaty was signed in 1949 the international situation has changed significantly and the political tasks of the Alliance have assumed a new dimension. Amongst other developments, the Alliance has played a major part in stopping Communist expansion in Europe; the USSR has become one of the two world super powers but the Communist world is no longer monolithic; the Soviet doctrine of "peaceful co-existence" has changed the nature of the confrontation with the West but not the basic problems. Although the disparity between the power of the United States and that of the European states remains, Europe has recovered and is on its way towards unity. The process of decolonisation has transformed European relations with the rest of the world; at the same time, major problems have arisen in the relations between developed and developing countries.

5. The Atlantic Alliance has two main functions. Its first function is to maintain adequate military strength and political solidarity to deter aggression and other forms of pressure and to defend the territory of member countries if aggression should occur. Since its inception, the Alliance has successfully fulfilled this task. But the possibility of a crisis cannot be excluded as long as the central political issues in Europe, first and foremost the German Question, remain unsolved. Moreover, the situation of instability and uncertainty still precludes a balanced reduction of military forces. Under these conditions, the Allies will maintain as necessary, a

---

Annexed to the Final Communique issued by the NATO Foreign Ministers following their meeting in Brussels, Belgium, on December 13-14, 1967.

suitable military capability to assure the balance of forces, thereby creating a climate of stability, security and confidence.

In this climate the Alliance can carry out its second function, to pursue the search for progress towards a more stable relationship in which the underlying political issues can be solved. Military security and a policy of détente are not contradictory but complimentary. Collective defence is a stabilising factor in world politics. It is the necessary condition for effective policies directed towards a greater relaxation of tensions. The way to peace and stability in Europe rests in particular on the use of the Alliance constructively in the interest of détente. The participation of the USSR and the USA will be necessary to achieve a settlement of the political problems in Europe.

6. From the beginning the Atlantic Alliance has been a co-operative grouping of states sharing the same ideals and with a high degree of common interest. Their cohesion and solidarity provide an element of stability within the Atlantic area.

7. As sovereign states the Allies are not obliged to subordinate their policies to collective decision. The Alliance affords an effective forum and clearing house for the exchange of information and views; thus, each Ally can decide its policy in the light of close knowledge of the problems and objectives of the others. To this end the practice of frank and timely consultations needs to be deepened and improved. Each Ally should play its full part in promoting an improvement in relations with the Soviet Union and the countries of Eastern Europe, bearing in mind that the pursuit of détente must not be allowed to split the Alliance. The chances of success will clearly be greatest if the Allies remain on parallel courses, especially in matters of close concern to them all; their actions will thus be all the more effective.

8. No peaceful order in Europe is possible without a major effort by all concerned. The evolution of Soviet and East European policies gives ground for hope that those governments may eventually come to recognize the advantages to them of collaborating in working towards a peaceful settlement. But no final and stable settlement in Europe is possible without a solution of the German question which lies at the heart of present tensions in Europe. Any such settlement must end the unnatural barriers between Eastern and Western Europe, which are most clearly and cruelly manifested in the division of Germany.

9. Accordingly the Allies are resolved to direct their energies to this purpose by realistic measures designed to further a détente in East-West relations. The relaxation of tensions is not the final goal but is part of a long-term process to promote better relations and to foster a European settlement. The ultimate political purpose of the Alliance is to achieve a just and lasting peaceful order in Europe accompanied by appropriate security guarantees.

10. Currently, the development of contacts between the countries of Western and Eastern Europe is mainly on a bilateral basis. Certain subjects, of course, require by their very nature, a multilateral solution.

11. The problem of German reunification and its relationship to a European settlement has normally been dealt with in exchanges between the Soviet Union and the three Western powers having special responsibilities in this field. In the preparation of such exchanges the Federal Republic of Germany has regularly joined the three Western powers in order to reach a common position. The other Allies will continue to have their views considered in timely discussions among the Allies about Western policy on this subject, without in any way impairing the special responsibilities in question.

12. The Allies will examine and review suitable policies designed to achieve a just and stable order in Europe, to overcome the division of Germany and to foster European security. This will be part of a process of active and constant preparation for the time when fruitful discussions of these complex questions may be possible bilaterally or multilaterally between Eastern and Western nations.

13. The Allies are studying disarmament and practical arms control measures, including the possibility of balanced force reductions. These studies will be intensified. Their active pursuit reflects the will of the Allies to work for an effective détente with the East.

14. The Allies will examine with particular attention the defence problems of the exposed areas e.g., the South-Eastern flank. In this respect the present situation in the Mediterranean presents special problems, bearing in mind that the current crisis in the Middle-East falls within the responsibilities of the United Nations.

15. The North Atlantic Treaty area cannot be treated in isolation from the rest of the world. Crises and conflicts arising outside the area may impair its security either directly or by affecting the global balance. Allied countries contribute individually within the United Nations and other international organisations to the maintenance of international peace and security and to the solution of important international problems. In accordance with established usage the Allies, or such of them as wish to do so, will also continue to consult on such problems without commitment and as the case may demand.

16. In the light of these findings, the Ministers directed the Council in permanent session to carry out, in the years ahead, the detailed follow-up resulting from this study. This will be done either by intensifying work already in hand or by activating highly specialized studies by more systematic use of experts and officials sent from capitals.

17. Ministers found that the study by the Special Group confirmed the importance of the role which the Alliance is called upon to play during the coming years in the promotion of détente and the strengthening of peace. Since significant problems have not yet been examined in all their aspects, and other problems of no less significance which have arisen from the latest political and strategic developments have still to be examined, the Ministers have directed the Permanent Representatives to put in hand the study of these problems without delay, following such procedures as shall be deemed most appropriate by the Council in permanent session, in order to enable further reports to be subsequently submitted to the Council in Ministerial Session.

Reykjavik Declaration on Mutual Force Reductions

1. Meeting at Reykjavik on 24th and 25th June, 1968, the Ministers recalled the frequently expressed and strong desire of their countries to make progress in the field of disarmament and arms control.

2. Ministers recognized that the unresolved issues which still divide the European Continent must be settled by peaceful means, and are convinced that the ultimate goal of a lasting, peaceful order in Europe requires an atmosphere of trust and confidence and can only be reached by a step-by-step process. Mindful of the obvious and considerable interest of all European States in this goal, Ministers expressed their belief that measures in this field including balanced and mutual force reductions can contribute significantly to the lessening of tension and to further reducing the danger of war.

3. Ministers noted the important work undertaken within the North Atlantic Council by member governments in examining possible proposals for such reductions pursuant to paragraph 13 of the "Report on the Future Tasks of the Alliance", approved by the Ministers in December 1967. In particular, they have taken note of the work being done in the Committee of Political Advisers to establish bases of comparison and to analyse alternative ways of achieving a balanced reduction of forces, particularly in the Central part of Europe.

4. Ministers affirmed the need for the Alliance to maintain an effective military capability and to assure a balance of forces between NATO and the Warsaw Pact. Since the security of the NATO countries and the prospects for mutual force reductions would be weakened by NATO reductions alone, Ministers affirmed the proposition that the overall military capability of NATO should not be reduced except as part of a pattern of mutual force reductions balanced in scope and timing.

5. Accordingly, Ministers directed Permanent Representatives to continue and intensify their work in accordance with the following agreed principles:

a. Mutual force reductions should be reciprocal and balanced in scope and timing.

b. Mutual reductions should represent a substantial and significant step, which will serve to maintain the present degree of security at reduced cost, but should not be such as to risk de-stabilizing the situation in Europe.

c. Mutual reductions should be consonant with the aim of creating confidence in Europe generally and in the case of each party concerned.

Declaration attached to the Final Communique issued by the NATO Foreign Ministers and representatives of countries participating in the NATO Defense Program, following their meeting in Reykjavik, Iceland, on June 24-25, 1968.

d. To this end, any new arrangement regarding forces should be consistent with the vital security interests of all parties and capable of being carried out effectively.

6. Ministers affirmed the readiness of their governments to explore with other interested states specific and practical steps in the arms control field.

7. In particular, Ministers agreed that it was desirable that a process leading to mutual force reductions should be initiated. To that end they decided to make all necessary preparations for discussions on this subject with the Soviet Union and other countries of Eastern Europe and they call on them to join in this search for progress towards peace.

8. Ministers directed their Permanent Representatives to follow up on this declaration.

Final Communique and Declaration of December 1969

Final Communique

1. The North Atlantic Council met in Ministerial Session at Brussels on 4th and 5th December, 1969. The meeting was attended by Foreign, Defence and Finance Ministers.

2. Since the signing of the North Atlantic Treaty twenty years ago, the members of the Alliance have dedicated their efforts to the preservation of their freedom and security and to the improvement of East-West relations in the aim of reaching an ultimate peaceful solution of outstanding problems in Europe. They will continue to do so.

3. By approving in December 1967 the Report on the Future Tasks of the Alliance, the Allied Governments resolved to maintain adequate military strength and political solidarity to deter aggression and other forms of pressure and to defend the territory of member countries if aggression should occur; and to examine suitable policies designed to achieve a just and stable order in Europe, to overcome the division of Germany and to foster European security.

4. On the basis of these two concepts of defence and the relaxation of tensions, the Ministers issued the Declaration attached to this Communiqué in which they set forth their views on the future development of relations between Eastern and Western countries.

5. Ministers welcomed the opening of Strategic Arms Limitation Talks. They acknowledged the work in progress with regard to arms control on the sea bed, as well as the interest shown both by the Conference of the Committee on Disarmament and the United Nations in measures to deal with chemical and biological warfare. On all these questions the Council held detailed consultations which proved most useful in preparing the ground for the negotiations taking place elsewhere. The Ministers invited the Council in Permanent Session to continue to examine these problems, and reaffirmed the importance of any genuine disarmament measure, consistent with the security of all states and guaranteed by adequate international control, for the reduction of tension and the consolidation of peace in Europe and the world.

6. The Ministers also studied a report by the Secretary General on the situation in the Mediterranean. Recalling the Communiqués issued on 27th June, 1968 and 16th November, 1968, they expressed the concern of their

---

Issued by the NATO Foreign Ministers following their meeting in Brussels, Belgium on December 4-5, 1969.

governments with regard to the situation in that area. The Ministers reaffirmed the value of full consultations among the Allies on this question. Accordingly, they requested the Council in permanent Session to pursue with the greatest attention its examination of the situation in the Mediterranean and to report to Ministers at their Spring Meeting.

7. In April 1969, Ministers called attention to the role the Alliance might play in tackling common environmental problems that could imperil the welfare and progress of modern societies. Consequently, the Council in Permanent Session established a Committee on the Challenges of Modern Society. The new Committee, beginning with its first meeting on 8th December, will address these urgent problems with the aim of stimulating action by members of the Alliance, either singly, jointly or in international organizations. The Ministers at their Spring Meeting will receive the Committee's first report on the newest task of the Alliance.

8. Ministers of countries participating in NATO's integrated defence programme met as the Defence Planning Committee on 3rd December, 1969. As an introduction to their discussions the Secretary General and the Chairman of the Military Committee gave overall appraisals of the state of defence planning within the Alliance. Ministers thereafter reviewed the work accomplished since their previous meeting on 28th May, 1969, and gave directions for future work.

9. They agreed that the effectiveness of NATO's defensive posture continues to be an essential stabilising factor in support of the search for meaningful détente. Therefore, until agreement can be reached on East-West mutual force reductions, balanced in scope and timing so as to maintain the present degree of security, NATO will continue to ensure that there is no reduction in its overall military capability.

10. In reviewing Force Plans for 1970, Ministers were conscious of the necessity to maintain adequate and readily available forces both conventional and nuclear, in accordance with the NATO strategy, for the defence of the mainland of Europe and the whole NATO area. They took note of the positive outcome of consultations with the Canadian Authorities, concerning their forces for NATO, which were initiated following the Defence Planning Committee meeting of 28th May, 1969. Ministers committed forces for the year 1970 and endorsed a number of remedial measures necessary to maintain adequate forces in Central Europe; in addition further remedial measures are under consideration.

11. They discussed measures required to implement the NATO strategy of forward defence based on flexibility in response, and arrangements for the reinforcement, in times of tension, of NATO's ready forces. They also noted a preliminary report on a comprehensive study which is being undertaken of the relative capabilities of the forces of NATO and the Warsaw Pact and gave

instructions for the continuance of the study. In addition, Ministers reviewed the status of other defence planning studies including those for improved defence of the flanks.

12. The Ministerial Meeting also provided the Defence Ministers comprising the Nuclear Defence Affairs Committee (Belgium, Canada, Denmark, Germany, Greece, Italy, Netherlands, Norway, Portugal, Turkey, the United Kingdom and the United States) with the occasion to review work in progress in the Nuclear Planning Group during the past year and planned for the future. The Nuclear Defence Affairs Committee agreed that Canada, Germany, Italy, Netherlands, Norway, Turkey, the United Kingdom and the United States will compose the Nuclear Planning Group starting 1st January, 1970.

13. Acting on the recommendation of the Nuclear Defence Affairs Committee, the Defence Planning Committee adopted two policy documents originated by the Nuclear Planning Group at their meeting in the United States last November concerning general guidelines for nuclear consultation procedure and for the possible tactical use of nuclear weapons in defence of the Treaty area. These documents are based upon NATO's strategy of flexibility in response which was adopted in December 1967 and which remains unchanged.

14. The next Ministerial Meeting of the Defence Planning Committee will take place in the Spring of 1970.

15. The Spring Ministerial Meeting of the Council will be held in Italy on 26th and 27th May, 1970.

Declaration

1. Meeting at Brussels on 4th and 5th December, 1969, the Ministers of the North Atlantic Alliance reaffirmed the commitment of their nations to pursue effective policies directed towards a greater relaxation of tensions in their continuing search for a just and durable peace.

2. Peace and security in Europe must rest upon universal respect for the principles of sovereign equality, political independence and the territorial integrity of each European state; the right of its peoples to shape their own destinies; the peaceful settlement of disputes; non-intervention in the internal affairs of any state by any other state, whatever their political or social system; and the renunciation of the use of the threat of force against any state. Past experience has shown that there is, as yet, no common interpretation of these principles. The fundamental problems in Europe can be solved only on the basis of these principles and any real and lasting improvement of East-West relations presupposes respect for them without any conditions or reservations.

3. At their meeting in Washington in April 1969, Ministers had expressed the intention of their governments to explore with the Soviet Union and the other countries of Eastern Europe which concrete issues best lend themselves to fruitful negotiation and an early resolution. To this end, the Council has been engaged in a detailed study of various issues for exploration and possible negotiation. Ministers recognized that procedure merited closer examination and, accordingly, requested the Council in Permanent Session to report to the next Ministerial Meeting.

4. Ministers considered that, in an era of negotiation, it should be possible, by means of discussion of specific and well-defined subjects, progressively to reduce tensions. This would in itself facilitate discussion of the more fundamental questions.

Arms Control and Disarmament

5. Ministers again expressed the interest of the Alliance in arms control and disarmament and recalled the Declaration on mutual and balanced force reductions adopted at Reykjavik in 1968 and reaffirmed in Washington in 1969. The Members of the Alliance have noted that up to now this suggestion has led to no result. The Allies, nevertheless, have continued, and will continue, their studies in order to prepare a realistic basis for active exploration at an early date and thereby establish whether it could serve as a starting point for fruitful negotiations. They requested that a report of the Council in Permanent Session on the preparation of models for mutual and balanced force reductions be submitted as soon as possible.

6. Ministers of countries participating in NATO's integrated defence programme consider that the studies on mutual and balanced force reductions have progressed sufficiently to permit the establishment of certain criteria which, in their view, such reductions should meet. Significant reductions under adequate verification and control would be envisaged under any agreement on mutual and balanced force reductions, which should also be consistent with the vital security interests of all parties. This would be another concrete step in advancing "along the road of ending the arms race and of general and complete disarmament, including nuclear disarmament".

7. These Ministers directed that further studies should be given to measures which could accompany or follow agreement on mutual and balanced force reductions. Such measures could include advance notification of military movements and manoeuvres, exchange of observers at military manoeuvres and possibly the establishment of observation posts. Examination of the techniques and methods of inspection should also be further developed.

Germany and Berlin

8. The Ministers welcome the efforts of the governments of the United States, Great Britain, and France, in the framework of their special responsibility for Berlin and Germany as a whole, to gain the co-operation of the Soviet Union in improving the situation with respect to Berlin and free access to the city. The elimination of difficulties created in the past with respect to Berlin, especially with regard to access, would increase the prospects for serious discussions on the other concrete issues which continue to divide East and West. Furthermore, Berlin could play a constructive role in the expansion of the East-West economic relations if the city's trade with the East could be facilitated.

9. A just and lasting peace settlement for Germany must be based on the free decision of the German people and on the interests of European security. The Ministers are convinced that, pending such a settlement, the proposals of the Federal Republic for a modus vivendi between the two parts of Germany and for a bilateral exchange of declarations on the non-use of force or the threat of force would, if they receive a positive response, substantially facilitate co-operation between East and West on other problems. They consider that these efforts by the Federal Republic represent constructive steps toward relaxation of tension in Europe and express the hope that the governments will therefore take them into account in forming their own attitude toward the German question.

10. The Ministers would regard concrete progress in both these fields as an important contribution to peace in Europe. They are bound to attach great weight to the responses to these proposals in evaluating the prospects for negotiations looking toward improved relations and co-operation in Europe.

Economic, technical and cultural exchanges

11. Allied governments consider that not only economic and technical but also cultural exchanges between interested countries can bring mutual benefit and understanding. In these fields more could be achieved by freer movement of people, ideas and information between the countries of East and West.

12. The benefit of the Alliance's work in the field of human environment would be enhanced if it were to become the basis of broader co-operation. This could, and should, be an early objective, being one in which the Warsaw Pact governments have indicated an interest. Further co-operation could also be undertaken, for example, in the more specialised field of oceanography. More intensive efforts in such fields should be pursued either bilaterally, multilaterally or in the framework of existing international bodies comprising interested countries.

Perspectives for negotiations

13. The Ministers considered that the concrete issues concerning European security and co-operation mentioned in this Declaration are subjects lending themselves to possible discussions or negotiations with the Soviet Union and the other countries of Eastern Europe. The Allied governments will continue and intensify their contacts, discussions or negotiations through all appropriate channels, bilateral or multilateral, believing that progress is most likely to be achieved by choosing in each instance the means most suitable for the subject. Ministers therefore expressed their support for bilateral initiatives undertaken by the German Federal Government with the Soviet Union and other countries of Eastern Europe, looking toward agreements on the renunciation of force and the threat of force. Ministers expressed the hope that existing contacts will be developed so as to enable all countries concerned to participate in discussions and negotiations on substantial problems of co-operation and security in Europe with real prospects of success.

14. The Members of the Alliance remain receptive to signs of willingness on the part of the Soviet Union and other Eastern European countries to discuss measures to reduce tension and promote co-operation in Europe and to take constructive actions to this end. They have noted in this connection references made by these countries to the possibility of holding an early conference on European security. Ministers agreed that careful advance preparation and prospects of concrete results would in any case be essential. Ministers consider that, as part of a comprehensive approach, progress in the bilateral and multilateral discussions and negotiations which have already begun, or could begin shortly, and which relate to fundamental problems of European security, would make a major contribution to improving the political atmosphere in Europe. Progress in these discussions and negotiations would help to ensure the success of any eventual conference in which, of course, the North American members of the Alliance would participate, to discuss and negotiate substantial problems of co-operation and security in Europe.

15. The Ministers affirmed that, in considering all constructive possibilities, including a general conference or conferences, they will wish to assure that any such meeting should not serve to ratify the present division of Europe and should be the result of a common effort among all interested countries to tackle the problems which separate them.

C Warsaw Pact Documents

Bucharest Declaration of July 1966

The People's Republic of Bulgaria, the Czechoslovak Socialist Republic, the Hungarian People's Republic, the German Democratic Republic, the Polish People's Republic, the Socialist Republic of Rumania and the Union of Soviet Socialist Republics, the states which are parties to the Warsaw Treaty of Friendship, Cooperation and Mutual Assistance, represented at the meeting in Bucharest of the political consultative committee, adopt the following Declaration:

I

The safeguarding of a lasting peace and of security in Europe is in accord with the ardent desires of all peoples of the continent of Europe and is in the interests of universal peace. . . .

Now, two decades after the end of World War II, its consequences in Europe have not yet been liquidated, there is no German peace treaty and hotbeds of tension and abnormal situations in relations between states continue to exist.

The socialist states which signed the present Declaration believe that the elimination of this situation and the creation of firm foundations of peace and security in Europe assume that international relations proceeding from the renunciation of the threat of force or the use of force, and the need to settle international disputes only by peaceful means, should be based on the principles of sovereignty and national independence, equality and non-interference in domestic affairs and on respect of territorial inviolability.

The states of Europe should strive for the adoption of effective measures to prevent the danger of the start of an armed conflict in Europe and for the strengthening of European collective security. . . .

II

The growth of the forces which are coming out for the preservation and strengthening of peace is one of the determining features of the present international situation. . . .

Tendencies towards getting rid of the features of the cold war and the obstacles standing in the way of a normal development of European co-operation, for the settlement of outstanding issues through mutual

Abridged form of the "Declaration on Strengthening Peace and Security in Europe," issued by the political leaders of the seven active members of the Warsaw Pact Political Consultative Committee (Albania excluded) following their summit meeting in Bucharest, Rumania, on July 5-8, 1966; this translation is reproduced, with permission, from *Survival*, volume viii, number 9, September 1966, pages 289-294.

understanding, for the normalization of international life and the *rapprochement* of peoples are increasingly appearing and developing in Europe. This course is opposed by imperialist reactionary circles which, pursuing aggressive aims, strive to fan tensions and to poison relations between the European states.

A direct threat to peace in Europe and to the security of the European peoples is presented by the present policy of the United States of America. . . . The United States interferes in the domestic affairs of other states, violates the sacred right of every people to settle its own destiny, resorts to colonial repressions and armed intervention, hatches plots in various countries of Asia, Africa and Latin America, and everywhere supports reactionary forces and venal regimes that are hated by the peoples. There can be no doubt that the aims of the United States policy in Europe have nothing in common with the vital interests of the European peoples and the aim of European security.

The American ruling circles would like to impose their will on their allies in Western Europe and to make Western Europe an instrument of the United States global policy, which is based on the attempt to stop and even turn back the historic process of the national and social liberation of the peoples. Hence the attempts to involve some West European states in military ventures even in other parts of the world, and Asia in particular.

The United States aggressive circles, which have the support of the reactionary forces of Western Europe, are, with the help of the North Atlantic military bloc and the military machine created by it, trying further to deepen the division of Europe, to keep up the arms race, to increase international tensions and to impede the establishment and development of normal ties between the West European and East European states. . . .

The US policy in Europe, promoted during the post-war years, is the more dangerous for the European peoples in that it is increasingly based on collusion with the militaristic and revanchist forces of West Germany. These forces are openly pushing the United States to promote an even more dangerous course in Europe. This policy is reflected in the projected creation of a sort of alliance between the American imperialists and the West German revanchists.

The militaristic and revanchist circles of West Germany do not want to take the vital interests of the German people itself into account; they are pursuing aggressive aims which manifest themselves in all their actions – in the switching of the country's economic potential to military lines, in the creation of a Bundeswehr of 500,000 men, in the glorification of the history of German conquests and in the nurturing of hatred towards other peoples whose lands are again coveted by these circles in the Federal Republic of Germany.

At present the demand for the possession of nuclear weapons is the focal point of this policy. The creation in the Federal Republic of Germany of a scientific technical and industrial basis that would serve at a certain moment for the manufacture of their own atomic and nuclear bombs is being openly and secretly accelerated. By their joint efforts, the peace-loving countries and peoples have so far succeeded in delaying the creation of a NATO joint nuclear force which would give the Federal Republic of Germany access to nuclear weapons; but the plans for this have not been shelved.

The fundamental interests of all the peoples demand the renunciation of the plans for creating a NATO multilateral nuclear force. If, however, the NATO countries, acting contrary to the interests of peace, embark on a course of implementing the plans for creating a multilateral nuclear force or giving West Germany access to nuclear weapons in any form whatsoever, the member states of the Warsaw Treaty Organization would be compelled to carry out the defensive measures necessary to ensure their security.

The territorial claims of the West German revanchists must be emphatically rejected. They are absolutely inviolability of the existing frontiers between European states, including the frontiers of the sovereign German Democratic Republic, Poland and Czechoslovakia, is one of the main prerequisites for ensuring European security.

The states represented at the present meeting confirm their resolution to crush any aggression against them on the part of the forces of imperialism and reaction. For their part, the member states of the Warsaw Treaty Organization declare that they have no territorial claims whatever against a single state in Europe. The policy of revanchism and militarism, carried through by German imperialism, has always ended in fiasco. Given the present balance of forces in the world arena and in Europe, it is attended by irreparable consequences for the Federal Republic of Germany.

The interests of peace and security in Europe and throughout the world, like the interests of the German people, demand that the ruling circles of the Federal Republic of Germany take the real state of affairs in Europe into account, and this means that they take as their point of departure the existence of two German states, abandon their claims for the frontiers of Europe to be carved up again, abandon their claims to the right exclusively to represent the whole of Germany and their attempts to bring pressure to bear on states that recognize the German Democratic Republic, renounce the criminal Munich *diktat,* and acknowledge that it has been null and void from the very beginning. They must prove by deeds that they have really learned the lessons of history and that they will put an end to militarism and revanchism and will carry through a policy of the normalization of relations between states and the development of cooperation and friendship between peoples.

The German Democratic Republic, which is a major factor making for the safeguarding of peace in Europe, has addressed the government and Bundestag of the Federal Republic of Germany with constructive proposals: to renounce nuclear arms on a reciprocal basis, to reduce the armies of both German states, to assume a commitment not to use force against each other and to sit down at a conference table for a solution of the national problems of interest to both the German Democratic Republic and the Federal Republic of Germany which have developed. The government of the Federal Republic of Germany, however, evinces no interest in these proposals. The states which have signed this Declaration support this initiative of the German Democratic Republic.

Having examined all aspects of the present situation in Europe, the states represented at the meeting have drawn the conclusion that in Europe, where almost half the states are socialist, it is possible to prevent undesirable developments. The problem of European security can be solved by the joint efforts of the European states and all the public forces that are coming out for peace, irrespective of their ideological views and religious or other convictions. This task will be all the more successfully accomplished, the sooner the influence of those forces who would like to continue aggravating tension in the relations between European states is paralyzed. . . .

A major factor which increasingly complicates the carrying out of war gambles in Europe is the growth of the influence of these forces in the West European states which are aware of the need to rise above differences in political views and convictions and come out for a relaxation of international tension, for the comprehensive development of mutually advantageous relations between all the states of Europe without discrimination and for the complete independence of their countries and the maintenance of their national identity.

The states which have signed this Declaration note as a positive feature the presence of circles in the Federal Republic of Germany that come out against revanchism and militarism, which call for the establishment of normal relations with the countries of both the West and the East, including normal relations between both German states, and are pressing for a relaxation of international tension and the safeguarding of European security so that all Germans may enjoy the blessings of peace. . . .

III

The states that are signatories to this Declaration hold that measures for the strengthening of security in Europe can and should be taken, in the first instance, in the following main directions:

1. They call upon all European states to develop good-neighbourly relations on the basis of the principles of independence and national sovereignty, equality, non-interference in internal affairs and mutual advantage founded on the principles of peaceful co-existence between states with different social systems. Proceeding from this, they come out for the strengthening of economic and trade relations, the multiplication of contacts and forms of co-operation in science, technology, culture and art, as well as in other areas which provide new opportunities for co-operation among European countries. . . .

The development of general European co-operation makes it necessary for all states to renounce any kind of discrimination and pressure, either political or economic in nature, designed against other countries, and requires their equal co-operation and the establishment of normal relations between them, including the establishment of normal relations with both German states. The establishment and development of good-neighbourly relations between European states with different social systems can make their economic and cultural contacts more active and thus increase the possibilities for European states to make an effective contribution to improving the climate in Europe and the development of mutual confidence and respect.

2. The socialist countries have always and consistently come out against the division of the world into military blocs or alliances, and for the elimination of the dangers which flow from this for universal peace and security. The Warsaw Treaty of Friendship, Co-operation and Mutual Assistance — a defensive pact of sovereign and equal states — was concluded in reply to the formation of the military aggressive NATO alignment and the inclusion of West Germany into it. However, the member states of the Warsaw Treaty Organization have considered and consider now that the existence of military blocs and war bases on the territories of other states, which are imposed by the imperialist forces, constitute an obstacle along the road of co-operation between states.

A genuine guarantee of the security and progress of every European country must be the establishment of an effective security system in Europe, based on relations of equality and mutual respect between all states of the continent and on the joint efforts of all European nations — and not the existence of military alignments which do not conform with healthy tendencies in international affairs today. The countries that have signed this Declaration consider that the need has matured for steps to be taken towards the relaxation, above all, of military tension in Europe.

The governments of our states have more than once pointed out that in case of the discontinuance of the operation of the North Atlantic Alliance, the Warsaw Treaty would become invalid, and that their place ought to be taken by a European security system. They now solemnly reaffirm their readiness for the simultaneous abolition of these alliances.

If, however, the member states of the North Atlantic Treaty are still not ready to accept the complete dissolution of both alignments, the states that have signed this Declaration consider that it is already now expedient to reach an understanding on the abolition of the military organization, both of the North Atlantic Pact and of the Warsaw Treaty. At the same time, they declare that as long as the North Atlantic bloc exists, and aggressive imperialist circles encroach on world peace, the socialist countries represented at this meeting, maintaining high vigilance, are fully resolved to strengthen their might and defence potential. At the same time, we believe it necessary that all member states of the North Atlantic Pact and the Warsaw Treaty, and also the countries who do not participate in any military alliances, should exert efforts on a bilateral or multilateral basis with the object of advancing the cause of European security.

3. Great importance is ow also assumed by such partial measures towards military relaxation on the European continent as the abolition of foreign war bases; the withdrawal of all forces from foreign territories to within their national frontiers; the reduction, on an agreed scale and at agreed deadlines, of the numerical strength of the armed forces of both German states; measures aimed at eliminating the danger of nuclear conflict (the setting up of nuclear-free zones and the assumption of the commitment by the nuclear powers not to use these weapons against the states which are parties to such zones, etc.); and the ending of flights by foreign planes carrying atom or hydrogen bombs over the territories of European states and of the entry of foreign submarines and surface ships with nuclear arms on board into the ports of such states.

4. The states must concentrate their efforts on excluding the possibility of access of the Federal Republic of Germany to nuclear weapons in any form — directly, or indirectly through alignments of states — and to exclusive control or any form of participation in the control of such weapons. The way this problem is resolved will largely determine the future of the peoples of Europe, and not only the peoples of Europe. On this question, too, half-hearted decisions are impermissible.

5. The immutability of frontiers is the foundation of a lasting peace in Europe. The interests of the normalization of the situation in Europe demand that all states, both in Europe and outside the European continent, proceed in their foreign political actions from recognition of the frontiers that really exist between European states, including the Polish frontier on the Oder-Neisse line and the frontiers between the two German states.

6. A German peace settlement is in accord with the interests of peace in Europe. The socialist states which are represented at the meeting are ready to continue the search for the solution of this problem. This solution must take into consideration the interests of the security of all the countries concerned and the security of Europe as a whole.

A constructive approach to this question is only possible if it proceeds from reality, above all, from recognition of the fact of the existence of two German states – the German Democratic Republic and the Federal Republic of Germany. At the same time, such a settlement requires recognition of the existing frontiers and the refusal of both German states to possess nuclear weapons. . . .

As for the reunion of both German states, the way to this lies through the relaxation of tension, through a gradual *rapprochement* between the two sovereign German states and agreements between them, through agreements on disarmament in Germany and Europe, and on the basis of the principle that when Germany is reunited, the united German state would be truly peaceful and democratic and would never again be a danger to its neighbors or to peace in Europe.

7. Convocation of a general European conference to discuss the questions of ensuring security in Europe and organizing general European co-operation would be of great positive importance. The agreement reached at the conference could be expressed, for example, in the form of a general European declaration on co-operation for the maintenance and strengthening of European security. Such a declaration could provide for an undertaking by the signatories to be guided in their relations by the interests of peace, to settle disputes by peaceful means only, to hold consultations and exchange information on questions of mutual interest and to contribute to the all-round development of economic, scientific, technical and cultural relations. The declaration should be open to all interested states to join.

The convocation of a conference on questions of European security and co-operation could contribute to the establishment of a system of collective security in Europe and would be an important landmark in the contemporary history of Europe. Our countries are ready to take part in such a conference at any time convenient to the other interested states, both members of the North Atlantic Treaty and neutrals. Neutral European countries could also play a positive role in the convocation of such a meeting. It goes without saying that the agenda and other questions concerning the preparation of such a meeting or conference should be decided upon by all participating states together, bearing in mind the proposals submitted by every one of them.

The countries represented at this meeting are also prepared to use other methods available for discussing problems of European security: talks through diplomatic channels, meetings of Foreign Ministers or special representatives on a bilateral or multilateral basis and contacts at the highest level. They consider that the considerations above cover the principal, the most important, aspects of ensuring European security. They are also ready to discuss other proposals which have been submitted, or may be submitted by any state, for the solution of this problem. . . . The parties to this meeting are convinced that countries on the other continents, too, cannot be indifferent to how things develop in Europe.

Karlovy Vary Statement of April 1967

We representatives of European Communist and Workers' Parties, who gathered in Karlovy Vary, realize our responsibility for the future of our peoples and the cause of the international working class and believe that preservation of peace is the most important question for all the peoples of our continent. We met to discuss the present situation, to exchange experience and jointly work out ways and means to help unite all forces of peace and progress in the struggle for European security.

I

The experience of the last few years has borne out the correctness of the Communists' thesis that world war is not inevitable and that it can be averted by the joint efforts of the world socialist community, the international working class, the national liberation movement and all States opposed to war, all peace forces. These forces have grown considerably, but the aggressiveness of American imperialism has also increased.

The United States, the main force of aggression and reaction, is trying to reverse the march of history and wipe out the right of the peoples to decide their destinies themselves. It is grossly interfering in the home affairs of countries in Latin America, Asia and Africa, and is extending its war of aggression against the Vietnamese people, a war which represents today the most serious danger to world peace.

In this situation the struggle against the imperialist forces is taking on special significance in Europe. Every success in this struggle means not only a step towards a stable peace in this part of the world but also a new blow at the policy of strength and the system of inter-connected aggressive military pacts with which imperialism has girdled the globe all over.

Europe, which lived through two world wars, remains a troubled region where the main forces of the imperialist camp and the socialist community are confronting each other. An armed conflict between them would threaten to grow into a total nuclear war. This danger is hanging over the entire life of the European peoples, it retards social and economic progress, vitiates international relations and involves tremendous loss of material means in the course of the arms race. Military intervention by certain European States to suppress the national liberation movements also creates hotbeds of tension and imperils peace.

Issued by the Conference of European Communist and Workers' Parties, held in Karlovy Vary (formerly Karlsbad), Czechoslovakia, on April 24-26, 1967; this translation is reproduced, with permission, from *Survival,* volume ix, number 7, July 1967, pages 208-213.

After the Second World War the imperialist nations, headed by the United States, concluded the North Atlantic Pact, spearheaded against the socialist States, and also against the democratic movements in the capitalist countries. This brought about the division of Europe into counterposed military blocs. Having remilitarized the German Federal Republic and supported its unlawful claims to represent all of Germany, the imperialists assigned it the role of an advanced anti-Communist bastion, which became a seat of tension and which threatens peace and security in Europe as a whole. The Bonn State, where revenge-seeking and militarist forces have come to power, has turned into the mainstay of United States global strategy in Europe.

The growing strength of the Bundeswehr, which is commanded by former Hitlerite officers, testifies to the increasing scope of military preparations. Activities of the Communist Party of Germany have been banned in the German Federal Republic, while other democratic and peace-loving organizations are being subjected to repressions. Broad scope is being given at the same time to the activities of extremely reactionary and neo-fascist forces. Their growing influence deeply alarms the European public, which is taught by painful experience that fascism is always accompanied by aggressive militarism.

The cold war has become for the monopolies of all the European capitalist States an instrument of waging an offensive against democracy, a tool for exerting pressure on the working people with a view to suppressing their struggle for better living conditions, for restricting their social gains, a means of shifting the growing burden of armaments on to the popular masses.

The cold war conceptions, the myth of the menace of 'communist aggression' used by the United States to justify its hegemony in Europe, have failed. The aggressive course of imperialism was undermined by the active foreign policy of the socialist States which are consistently implementing the principle of the peaceful coexistence of States with different social systems, a policy which is being carried through on an ever greater scale, especially since the 20th Congress of the CPSU. This course was also undermined by the struggle of Communist and Workers' Parties, the actions of the masses, the activity of broad sections of the West European public. The joint defensive might of the socialist States, which relies above all on the technical and scientific achievements of the Soviet Union, constitutes an obstacle in the way of war.

The Atlantic bloc has entered a stage of open crisis. The ruling quarters of some Western countries challenge the value and expediency of the policy of military alliance with the United States or participation in the NATO joint armed forces, which threatens to draw their States into war and has nothing in common with their national interests. Tendencies towards emancipation from political and military trusteeship by the United States are growing in the European capitalist countries. At the same time anxiety is growing over the intensifying penetration by American capital.

The contradictions have also been aggravated between the national interests of West European States and the expansionist aims of the German Federal Republic, its desire to occupy a dominating position in NATO, the Common Market and Euratom.

The German Democratic Republic, which has carried out the Potsdam agreements, has strengthened its sovereignty as a State and its international prestige. Its growing strength and constructive peace policy raise a barrier to the plans of West German imperialism. Recognition of the GDR and defence of its sovereign rights have become one of the main tasks in the struggle for European security. The existence and development of a peaceful socialist German State has great implications not only for the German people but also for peace all over Europe.

The crisis of the cold war policy has opened up new opportunities for the democratic and progressive forces existing in West Germany, forces that sincerely demand radical changes of the foreign policy and which deserve every kind of support. Replacement of the Bonn Government was brought about precisely by this crisis. However, there are no signs the new Government of the so-called Big Coalition has abandoned the imperialist goals of its predecessors. On the contrary, despite assurances of peaceful designs, it upholds claims to represent all of Germany, continues to strive to swallow up the GDR, to restore Germany within the frontiers of 1937, refuses to recognize the unlawfulness of the Munich *diktat*, continues to advance provocative claims to West Berlin, is striving to get access to nuclear arms.

Serious changes are now taking place in public opinion. The awareness of the fruitlessness and danger of the imperialist policy of splitting Europe is constantly growing. Ties of co-operation, specifically in the fields of economy and culture, are developing between countries with different social systems. In the course of establishing relations, representatives of governmental and public circles of socialist and capitalist countries carry out a useful exchange of views on problems of European security.

The constructive proposals for the strengthening of security and peaceful co-operation in Europe, set out by the socialist countries in the Bucharest Declaration of Warsaw Treaty States, and the proposals of the Communist parties of capitalist countries put forward at their meetings and in their decisions provide a realistic basis for the strengthening of peace and security in Europe. New and positive trends towards an international *détente* and co-operation with Communists are appearing in the socialist and the social-democratic movements in some West European countries. New trends are emerging in Christian circles as regards problems of progress and peace. New possibilities have arisen for contacts and co-operation between various trade union and other democratic organizations. Co-operation of Communists with socialists and believers in the question of European security can promote the cause of peace on our continent.

The peoples of Europe want no other war! They want neither a cold war nor a 'balance of fear' which leads to a still more intense arms race and increases the risk of a deliberate or accidental conflict. It is high time to achieve the establishment of new relations in Europe, resting on a genuine relaxation of tension and mutual confidence.

We Communists, acting in different national conditions, will stint no effort to build a system of collective security, to establish such relations between States which would preclude any possibility of aggression and ensure an enduring peace in Europe and throughout the world. This is a difficult, but feasible task.

II

The Communist and Workers' Parties of Europe are submitting for the consideration of public opinion and of all the political and public forces concerned a programme of activities in the interests of creating a system of collective security, based on principles of peaceful co-existence between countries with different social systems. This requires, primarily, that all States should recognize the actually existing situation as it has developed in Europe in the post-war period. This means:

—recognition of the inviolability of the existing frontiers in Europe, particularly on the Oder and the Neisse, and also of the borders between both German States;

—recognition of the existence of two sovereign and equal German States, the German Democratic Republic and the German Federal Republic, which requires of the latter the renunciation of its claim to represent the whole of Germany;

—exclusion of any opportunity for the German Federal Republic to gain access to nuclear arms in any form, either European, multilateral or Atlantic;

—recognition of the Munich treaty as invalid since the moment of its conclusion.

The European and working class movement and all democratic peace forces are now facing the task of ensuring the development of peaceful relations and co-operation among all European States on the basis of respect for their sovereignty and equality. With these aims in view it is necessary to fight for the realization of a number of aims which can be achieved in a new situation, namely:

—Conclusion by all European States of a treaty renouncing the use of force or threat of force in their relations, and interference in internal affairs; a treaty guaranteeing the solution of all disputes by peaceful means only, in accordance with the principles of the UN Charter.

—Normalization of relations between all States and the GDR, as also between both German States and between the GDR and West Berlin as a separate political entity.

—Consistent defence and development of democracy in the German Federal Republic — the right to demand this is given to the peoples by law, historical experience, and post-war international agreements. This envisages universal support for the struggle of the German Federal Republic's progressive forces for the banning of neo-Nazi organizations and all revenge-seeking propaganda, annulment of the emergency legislation, freedom of activity of the democratic and peace-loving forces, lifting of the ban on the Communist Party of Germany.

—Conclusion of a non-proliferation treaty as an important step towards the stopping of the arms race.

The system of European security must contain a recognition of the principle of neutrality and unconditional respect of the inviolability of neutral States. A more active peace-loving policy of these countries and their contribution to the cause of disarmament would help to establish such a system.

Liquidation of artificially created barriers in economic relations between the socialist and capitalist States of Europe would be of particular importance for all States and would be conducive to the establishment of fruitful co-operation, including broad agreements in the sphere of production and scientific research.

Striving to open a prospect to European security and co-operation, we are resolutely coming out for the conclusion of agreements on partial solutions, above all, in the sphere of disarmament, which would create a favourable climate for more far-reaching treaties. All proposals in this field, advanced by Governments, parties, public organizations, political leaders and scientists, deserve thorough examination. Particularly topical among these proposals are those which deal with the withdrawal of foreign troops from the territory of European States, liquidation of foreign war bases, establishment of denuclearized zones in Central Europe, in the Balkans, the territory of Danubian countries, in the Mediterranean and in Northern Europe, and also zones of thinned-out or frozen armaments and in general zones of peace and co-operation in various regions of the continent. These, just as other steps would check the tendency towards intensification of the arms race.

The 20-year period of validity of the Atlantic Pact expires in 1969, and this brings about a clear alternative: a Europe without military blocs. This alternative must be put on the agenda with all earnestness. No efforts should be spared in order to develop a wide-scale movement of the peace-loving forces of our continent against the extension or any modification of the Atlantic Pact. This movement is favoured by the constructive attitude of the Warsaw Treaty member nations which have repeatedly stated and solemnly confirmed in the Bucharest Declaration their readiness for a simultaneous liquidation of both military alliances. We second the moves of these States regarding an immediate agreement on the liquidation of the military organizations of the Atlantic Pact and the Warsaw Treaty.

We express readiness to support any initiatives or proposals pursuing the purpose of achieving a *détente* and strengthening the security of the peoples of our continent.

We fully support the proposal to call a conference of all European States on the question of security and peaceful co-operation in Europe. The proposal to call a conference of representatives of all the European parliaments also deserves support. Consolidation of security and peace will open up before the peoples of our continent new prospects for progress and prosperity.

The peoples of Europe are faced with important social, economic and cultural problems. A Europe, rid of the arms race, which consumes tremendous economic resources and the fruits of labour of workers, engineers and scientists, will be able not only to ensure higher living standards for its population, but also to make a valuable contribution to the development of all mankind.

Struggle for such a Europe is closely associated with struggle for genuine national independence, for democracy, against reactionary and fascist dictorships such as exist in Spain, Portugal and Greece. The fact that the Governments of Spain, Portugal and Greece assist American imperialism in building atomic bases in exchange for US support for these discredited regimes shows what a great danger they are to Europe. The European Communist and Workers' Parties express complete solidarity with and provide support to the important struggle that is now being waged by the united front of Spanish workers and democratic forces, and to all the peoples fighting against reactionary regimes, for freedom and democracy. The Communists who have always fought against imperialism, colonialism and neo-colonialism, will strengthen their solidarity with the peoples who are still fighting for national liberation. They will act for the development of new relations with the countries of Asia, Africa and Latin America, relations based on the principles of respect for national independence, sovereignty, non-interference in internal affairs, mutually profitable economic co-operation and effective aid by industrially highly developed countries to countries which have only recently become free and now follow the road of socio-economic and cultural progress.

III

The Communist and Workers' Parties of Europe are ready to dedicate all their forces to the realization of these tasks, serving the cause of peace, progress and democracy. Our movement which is marking this year the 50th anniversary of its great victory – the great October Socialist Revolution – has become a mighty political force, exerting a decisive influence on the development of all of mankind.

Each of the Communist Parties, in the specific conditions that it is fighting in, bears responsibility for its policy to the working class and the working people of its country, to the people in general. At the same time each part is aware of its international responsibility for the safeguarding of peace, for the formation of new international relations, conforming to the needs of our epoch.

This sense of responsibility requires of us, the Communist Parties of Europe, the pooling of our efforts for the solution of these problems. The stronger the unity and solidarity of the Communist and Workers' Parties in Europe and all over the world, the more effective our struggle shall be.

This sense of responsibility obliges us to address, primarily, all the working class, which is the main producer of material values, the most conscientious and progressive class of modern society. We address the closest ally of the working class, the peasantry, and also the middle classes, which are vitally interested in peace and prosperity. The workers and all the working people of Europe, combining patriotism with international fraternal solidarity, are capable of playing a decisive role in the struggle for peace and European security, for democracy and social progress in our continent.

We address the socialist and social democratic parties, which have a broad influence in the European working class and take part in the Governments of a number of European countries. The experience of decades has shown that joint actions by Communists and socialists enable the working class to exert a decisive influence on political life and rally around themselves public sections that are interested in the maintenance of peace and the implementation of democratic social changes.

We address the trade unions of Europe, which for 100 years have been the biggest mass organization of the working class, defending its material and social interests; we call upon the trade union organizations to use their authority and influence in the struggle for a peaceful Europe.

We address scientists, writers, artists, all European intellectuals, whose finest representatives have always defended human rights and freedoms, the independence of the peoples, and have supported international co-operation and peace.

We address the Christian forces, the Catholics and Protestants, the believers of all religious denominations who motivate their striving for peace and social justice by religious convictions.

We address the younger generation of Europe, whose future is inseparably bound up with victory of the idea of collective security and peace. The place of youth is in the first ranks of the fighters against the policy of war, against reaction and fascism, for freedom and progress, for friendship of the peoples.

We address the women whose role in social life is increasing all the time and whose participation in the defence of peace and the security of mankind is so important.

We address the bourgeois groupings, which display a realistic approach to modern reality, realize the danger of a nuclear war, wish to rid their countries of dependence on the United States and are ready to support the policy of European security.

We call upon all peace-loving forces to rally and launch a broad campaign in their countries and on a continental scale to expand direct actions for collective security. We urge support in every possible way for the proposal to call a conference of European nations.

The Communists of the European countries are deeply convinced that, by defending peace and security in their continent against the forces of aggression and war, they are acting in the interests of democracy, social progress and national liberation, in the interests of the peoples of all the world.

The present historical period requires courage and initiative. We address all the people of goodwill, irrespective of their political convictions and party membership, nationality or religion, with a call to use all their influence and exert every effort to achieve our common goal — peace. By overcoming all that divides us, we shall be able to create a mighty force, capable of triumphing over war and uncertainty in the morrow, of paving the way to a lasting peace and prosperity of the peoples.

The European peoples are capable of deciding themselves the questions of peace and security in their continent. Let them take the destinies of Europe into their own hands!

Communist Chinese Comment on the Karlovy Vary Conference

The Soviet revisionist leading clique dragged together a handful of its followers in Europe and convened a counter-revolutionary gangsters' meeting at Karlovy Vary, Czechoslovakia, from 24 to 26 April.

Brezhnev, Kosygin and company were busy a whole year plotting that meeting. Their blueprint called for a demonstrative four-day meeting to be held amid a flourish of trumpets, so as to give the modern revisionists a shot in the arm and a bit of a lift. But after just two and a half days, the meeting got bogged down. Brezhnev packed and left, and the meeting came to a hasty premature close.

This was a meeting symbolic of the utter bankruptcy of Europe's new scabs. Brezhnev, Kosygin and company took great pains to pull together a meeting. They travelled hither and yon and used soft and tough tactics at the same time. Nevertheless, attendance was poor and indifferent. Some parties disobeyed the baton of Soviet revisionism and refused to attend. The traitorous Tito clique also kept away because it wanted to maintain its 'special position' as a long-time flunkey of US imperialism.

The meeting was convened by the Soviet revisionists to engineer further actions against China. At the meeting, Brezhnev led the attack. Outside the meeting, the gang undertook intense anti-China activities. But few had the nerve to come forward and oppose China openly. Instead, they went out of their way to explain that the anti-China question 'does not form part of the agenda of our conference'. Why should something so queer happen? This was only an attempt to make the meeting more deceptive and to ward off exposure and criticism by the Marxist-Leninists and revolutionary people. It shows that the Soviet revisionists hit snags at the meeting when they openly tried to fly the flag of united action against China. This shows up the dilemma of the anti-China heroes who want to oppose China but find it not practical.

The Karlovy Vary meeting had been contemplated as preparatory to a massive assembly of all the renegades and scabs of the world which the Soviet revisionists have been trying to knock together. Brezhnev, Kosygin and company clamoured long ago about convening a 'new world conference of Communist Parties'. They put up quite a show with several of them speaking at once. Some said, 'Conditions are maturing'; others said, 'Conditions become increasingly mature'; still others, 'Conditions have matured'. But

This translation of the Communist Chinese comment was printed under the title "The Bankruptcy of Europe's New Scabs" in the *People's Daily* on May 4, 1967, and is reproduced, with permission, from *Survival,* volume ix, number 7, July 1967, pages 213-215.

these clamours were suddenly silenced at the Karlovy Vary meeting of scabs. Did they no longer intend to call such a conference to oppose Communism, China, the people, revolution and Marxism-Leninism, Mao Tse-tung's thought? That surely was not the case. The scabs kept mute on this question for their own ulterior motives. Each having his own calculations, they were beset with contradictions and found it hard to arrive at agreement.

Brezhnev, Kosygin and company had hoped that the meeting would help them restore the 'authority' of the baton of Khrushchev revisionism. Contrary to their hopes, the baton of Soviet revisionism became still less effective. The European revisionist cliques each manages his own business, and the tendency to act on one's own has been growing. Though they try their best to conceal it, they have to admit, however reluctantly, that there are 'differences' among them and it is 'not a simple and easy task' to work out a common policy.

The Karlovy Vary meetings revealed that although the European modern revisionists 'sleep in the same bed, they all have different dreams', each having his own axe to grind. They are divided and falling apart. This was a big exposure of the internal contradictions among the new European scabs.

The participants produced a statement with empty talk about 'peace in Europe' in abstract terms. They described the statement as a 'programme of action for peace and security in Europe'. Tass reported that, 'presided over by L. I. Brezhnev, the Conference unanimously approved the text of a statement "for peace and security in Europe".' In the eyes of Brezhnev, this 'unanimity', demonstrated under this chairmanship, was something to brag about. As a matter of fact, precisely the 'unanimity' they achieved on the question of peace revealed their true colours as a bunch of scabs. This is the same kind of 'unanimity' that Kautsky boasted about, referring to the second international renegades. Lenin said, 'To Kautsky, the unanimous desire of the Chauvinists who have betrayed socialism to deceive the workers, is proof of the 'unanimity' and viability of the international on the question of peace'. In using empty talk about 'peace' to benumb the revolutionary will of the working class, the new scabs, Brezhnev and company, exceeded even old renegades like Kautsky in brazenness.

On the question of European 'peace and security', the Karlovy Vary meeting fell back on a lot of hackneyed phrases, some picked up from the old revisionists, some from Khrushchev, some from Tito and some from the imperialists. This lengthy 7,000-word statement is crammed with deceitful phrases on what they call disarmament, the abolition of the two military blocs, the establishment of a European collective security system, European co-operation, a conference of European countries and united action with the socialist parties.

In the last analysis, this reactionary and hypocritical statement on 'peace and security in Europe' boils down to opposition to the proletarian revolution and the dictatorship of the proletariat and preservation in Europe of the rule of imperialism, capitalism and revisionism.

What Brezhnev, Kosygin and company call 'peace in Europe' means the 'peaceful' evolution of the socialist countries to capitalism, the 'peaceful' toleration by the working class in the capitalist countries of oppression and exploitation and the 'peaceful' degeneration of the Communist and Workers' Parties into new Social Democratic Parties.

What Brezhnev, Kosygin and company call 'security in Europe' means security for the privileged bourgeois stratum in the countries where the revisionist groups are in power, security for the reactionary ruling class in the imperialist and capitalist countries and the security of a handful of renegades and scabs in the Communist and Workers' Parties controlled by modern revisionist groups.

The Karlovy Vary Meeting was a meeting in the service of US imperialism. Desperately trying to maintain 'peace and security' in Europe, they aim at helping US imperialism 'stabilize' Europe, suppress the revolutionary movement of the world's people, suppress the national liberation movement in Asia, Africa and Latin America, in particular the vigorously developing national liberation movement in South-East Asia, and widen the war of aggression against Vietnam. The appeal issued by the Karlovy Vary meeting for 'aid' to Vietnam is a smoke-screen designed to cover up their counter-revolutionary purpose of serving US imperialism.

The Karlovy Vary meeting usurped the name of the 'Communist and Workers' Parties in Europe'. What kind of Communist Parties? The participants in the conference — the Brezhnev-Kosygin crowd of the Soviet Union, the Ulbricht crowd of East Germany, the Gomulka crowd of Poland, the Novotny crowd of Czechoslovakia, the Zhivko crowd of Bulgaria, the Janos Kadar crowd of Hungary, the Rochet crowd of France, the Longo crowd of Italy, the Gollan crowd of Britain, the Ibarruri crowd of Spain — all are renegades to Marxism-Leninism, scabs of the working class and enemies of the revolutionary Communist parties.

The Karlovy Vary meeting was a meeting of representatives of the privileged bourgeois stratum of the Soviet Union and East European countries and the agents of the bourgeoisie of some capitalist countries in Europe; it was a meeting at which the new Social Democratic Parties went a step farther in colluding with the old Social Democratic Parties. The new Social Democratic Parties and the old Social Democratic Parties in Europe have become a 'maintenance club' to keep all reactionary rule, reactionary systems and reactionary forces going a bit longer. The Karlovy Vary meeting reflected the fear and desperate death-bed struggle of the international bourgeoisie.

The Karlovy Vary meeting inherited Khrushchev revisionism and reaffirmed the capitulationist line of 'peaceful co-existence' of the 20th Congress of the CPSU in a vain attempt to prop up the tottering rule of imperialism and capitalism. But, no matter how hard Brezhnev, Kosygin and company try to serve imperialism, corrupt the working class and oppose and sabotage revolution, they cannot in any way save imperialism and capitalism from certain doom.

Comrade Mao Tse-tung has said: 'The socialist system will eventually replace the capitalist system; this is an objective law, independent of man's will. However much the reactionaries try to hold back the wheel of history, sooner or later revolution will take place and will inevitably triumph'.

Widespread dissemination of the great thought of Mao Tse-tung throughout the world, and the powerful impact of China's great proletarian cultural revolution upon the world, are giving further impetus to the revolutionary struggle of the peoples of Asia, Africa and Latin America and rousing the working class and labouring people of Europe, North America and Oceania to a new awakening.

Albania, the great beacon of socialism in Europe, shines in full radiance.

The Marxist-Leninist parties and organizations of various countries in Europe are growing stronger. We are convinced that these parties and organizations, under the guidance of Marxism-Leninism, Mao Tse-tung's thought, and by uniting with and leading the working class and labouring people of Europe, will be able to overthrow the reactionary rule of imperialism, capitalism and revisionism and achieve the complete liberation of their own people.

Budapest Appeal of March 1969

Communique

A meeting of the Political Consultative Committee of the member-countries of the Warsaw Treaty of Friendship, Co-operation and Mutual Assistance was held in Budapest on 17 March 1969.

The Political Consultative Committee heard a report from the Supreme Commander-in-Chief of the Joint Armed Forces on measures worked out by the Ministers of Defence with the approval of the respective governments.

The states taking part in the meeting thoroughly considered and unanimously endorsed the Statute on the Committee of Defence Ministers of the Warsaw Treaty Member-Countries, the new Statute on the Joint Armed Forces and the Joint Command and other documents designed to bring about a further improvement in the structure and organs of administration of the defence organization of the Warsaw Treaty.

The Supreme Commander-in-Chief of the Joint Armed Forces has been instructed to ensure the implementation of the decisions adopted, in conformity with the established procedure.

Those taking part in the meeting expressed their firm confidence that the steps approved would still further promote the strengthening of the defence potential of the socialist countries which are parties to the Warsaw Treaty, in the interests of the cause of socialism and the cause of peace and security in Europe and throughout the world.

Continuing their efforts aimed at securing a relaxation of tension and the consolidation of peace, the Warsaw Treaty member-countries unanimously adopted an address to all European countries concerning preparations for, and the holding of, a general European conference on questions of security and co-operation in Europe.

The meeting of the Political Consultative Committee was held in a spirit of fraternal friendship and comradely co-operation.

Call for European Conference

The People's Republic of Bulgaria, the Czechoslovak Socialist Republic, the German Democratic Republic, the Hungarian People's Republic, the Polish

---

Issued by the Party and state leaders of the seven active members of the Warsaw Pact Political Consultative Committee (Abania excluded) following their summit meeting in Budapest, Hungary, on March 17, 1969; this translation is reproduced, with permission, from *Survival*, volume xi, number 5, May 1969, pages 159161.

People's Republic, the Socialist Republic of Rumania and the Union of Soviet Socialist Republics, member-countries of the Warsaw Treaty and participants in the meeting of the Political Consultative Committee,

Expressing the aspirations of their peoples to live in peace and as good neighbours with the other European peoples, and also their firm determination to help to bring about an atmosphere of security and co-operation on our continent, address all European states with the following call to redouble their efforts aimed at strengthening peace and security in Europe.

The present and future of the peoples of Europe cannot be divorced from the preservation and consolidation of peace on our continent. Genuine security and reliable peace on our continent. Genuine security and reliable peace can be safeguarded if the thoughts, deeds and energies of the European states are directed towards the easing of tension, the solution of international problems that are ready for settlement, taking account of reality, and the establishment of all-round co-operation on a general European foundation.

The road to good neighbourliness, confidence and mutual understanding depends on the will and the efforts of the peoples and governments of all European countries. Present-day Europe, as it has emerged from World War II, means over 30 states, large and small, differing in their social systems, location and interests. By the will of history, they have been fated to live side by side, and no one can change this fact.

Ever more governments, parliaments, parties, political leaders and public figures are becoming aware of the responsibility they bear before the present and future generations to prevent another military conflict in Europe. However, forces are also continuing to operate in Europe which regard as assets for European development, not the settlement of disputes and peaceful agreements, but additional divisions and missiles, and fresh military programmes worked out for decades ahead. Operating together with them, there are also those who have not learnt the appropriate lessons from the outcome of World War II, as a result of which German militarism and nazism were routed. Their intrigues are a source of tension and complicate international relations.

The states taking part in the meeting regard it as their duty to continue doing their utmost to safeguard Europe from the danger of new military conflicts and to provide wide scope for the development of co-operation among all European countries, irrespective of their social systems, on the basis of the principles of peaceful co-existence.

No matter how complicated are the problems outstanding, they must be solved peacefully through talks, and not through the use of force or the threat of force. Examining the situation in Europe, the Warsaw Treaty member-countries consider that there are real opportunities for safeguarding

European security through common efforts, taking into account the interests of all the states and peoples of Europe.

Nearly three years ago, the Warsaw Treaty member-countries put forward in Bucharest a proposal for the convocation of a general European conference to discuss problems of European security and peaceful co-operation. Contacts maintained since that time have shown that not a single European government has opposed the idea of a general European conference and that there are real possibilities of holding it.

Since World War II the states of Europe have not yet met all together even once, although there are many questions that are awaiting discussion by them at a conference table. If one proceeds on the basis of the interests of strengthening peace, there are no weighty reasons whatsoever for postponing the convocation of a general European conference.

Such a conference would be in keeping with the interests of all European states. It would make it possible together to find ways and means which would lead to the ending of the division of Europe into military groupings and to the establishment of peaceful co-operation among the European states and peoples.

However, there are forces in the world which, seeking to maintain the division of our continent, pursuing a policy of fomenting tensions and rejecting the establishment of peaceful co-operation among states and peoples, oppose the calling of such a conference and other steps to strengthen European security.

The states taking part in this meeting are convinced that the development of general European co-operation has been and continues to be thy only real alternative to the dangerous military confrontation, the arms race and the dissensions which the aggressive forces, seeking to wreck the results of World War II and to carve up the map of Europe again, are trying to continue imposing upon Europe.

The Warsaw Treaty member-countries reaffirm their proposals directed against the division of the world into military blocs, the arms race and the danger to the cause of peace and security of the peoples ensuing from this, and the other steps and provisions contained in the Declaration on Strengthening Peace and Security in Europe, adopted in Bucharest in 1966.

It is a vital need for the European peoples to avert fresh military conflicts and to strengthen political, economic and cultural contacts among all states on the basis of equality and respect for the independence and sovereignty of states. A firm system of European security will create the objective possibility and necessity for implementing through joint efforts major projects in power engineering, transport, water and air space, and the health services, which have a direct bearing on the welfare of the population of the entire continent. It is precisely this common factor that can and must become a foundation for European co-operation.

One of the main preconditions for safeguarding European security is the inviolability of the frontiers existing in Europe, including the frontiers on the Oder and Neisse and also the frontiers between the German Democratic Republic and the Federal Republic of Germany, recognition of the existence of the German Democratic Republic and the Federal Republic of Germany, renunciation by the Federal Republic of Germany of its claims to represent the entire German people, and renunciation of the possession of nuclear weapons in any form. West Berlin has a special status and does not belong to West Germany.

A practical step towards strengthening European security would be a meeting at the earliest possible date, of representatives of all interested European states, to establish by mutual agreement the procedure for calling the conference and also to determine the items on its agenda. We are ready to consider at the same time any other proposal concerning the method for preparing and convening this conference.

The states taking part in the meeting of the Political Consultative Committee address all the countries of Europe with a call for co-operation in convening a general European conference and creating the necessary preconditions so that this conference may be successful and justify the hopes placed in it by the peoples.

In the interests of taking this important action, which would be an historic event in the life of the continent, the states taking part in the meeting address all European countries with a solemn call for strengthening the climate of confidence and, with this in view, to refrain from any actions that might poison the atmosphere in relations between states. They appeal for a change-over from general statements about peace to specific actions and measures for *détente* and disarmament and they call for the development of co-operation and peace among the peoples. They address all European governments with a call to pool their efforts so that Europe may become a continent of fruitful co-operation among equal nations, a factor for stability, peace and mutual understanding throughout the world.

[This address was signed by Todor Zhivkov for Bulgaria; Ludvik Svoboda, Alexander Dubcek and Oldrich Cernik for Czechoslovakia; Walter Ulbricht and Willi Stoph for the German Democratic Republic; Janos Kadar and Jenö Fock for Hungary; Wladyslaw Gomulka and Jozef Cyrankiewicz for Poland; Nicolae Ceausescu and Ion Gheorghe Maurer for Rumania; and Leonid Brezhnev and Alexei Kosygin for the Soviet Union.]

The Prague Communique of October 1969

On 30 and 31 October 1969 consultations took place in Prague by the Ministers of Foreign Affairs of the member-states of the Warsaw Treaty attended by the following: For the Bulgarian People's Republic: Mr. I. Duchev; for the Hungarian People's Republic: Mr. K. Erdelyi (Deputy Minister); for the German Democratic Republic: Mr. O. Winser; for the Polish People's Republic: Mr. S. Jodryehewski; for the Rumanian Socialist Republic: Mr. G. Manescu; for the Union of Soviet Socialist Republics: Mr. A. A. Gromyko; for the Czechoslovak Socialist Republic: Mr. J. Marko.

The governments represented at the consultations emphasized their efforts and willingness to undertake individually or in co-operation with other states new steps aimed at the relaxation of tension, strengthening of security and development of peaceful co-operation in Europe. They reaffirm the provisions of the Budapest Appeal of the participating Warsaw Treaty states to all European countries of 17 March 1969 which have proven their vitality.

The participants in the consultations paid special attention to the preparations for the convening of the All-European Conference on the Questions of Security and Co-operation in Europe. They noted with satisfaction that the proposal for the holding of the European Conference has met with a positive response on the part of most European states. In Europe the proposal has become a subject of active and matter-of-fact consideration in the course of which concrete ideas were advanced in regard of various questions relating to the preparation of the conference. This creates practical possibilities for the convening of the conference and for the achievement of European security through joint efforts in the interest of all states and people of Europe.

The valuable initiative taken by the Finnish Government of 5 May 1969, whereby it declared its willingness to assist in the preparation and holding of the All-European Conference was also welcomed with appreciation. All countries signatories of the Budapest Appeal responded in a positive manner.

The Ministers of Foreign Affairs of the Warsaw Treaty member-states acting on instructions of their governments propose that the following questions be included in the agenda of the All European Conference:

Issued by the Foreign Ministers of the seven active members of the Warsaw Pact (Albania excluded) following their consultative meeting held in Prague, Czechoslovakia, on October 30-31, 1969; this unofficial translation is reproduced, with permission, from *Survival,* volume xi, number 12, December 1969, pages 394-396.

1. The ensuring of European security and renunciation of the use of force or threat of its use in the mutual relations among states in Europe;

2. Expansion of trade, economic, scientific and technical relations on the principle of equal rights aimed at the development of political co-operation among European states.

The socialist states which signed this declaration are deeply convinced that a fruitful consideration of the above-mentioned questions and the reaching of agreement in that respect would facilitate a lessening of tension in Europe, growth of mutual understanding, development of peaceful and friendly relations among states and thereby the ensuring of security in which all European states are vitally interested. The success of the All-European Conference would constitute a historic event in the life of our continent and in the life of the nations all over the world. It would open up a way to the subsequent consideration of other problems of interest to European states whose solution would correspond to the strengthening of peace in Europe, assist in the development of broad, mutually beneficial co-operation among all European states and the ensuring of reliable security based on collective principles and joint efforts of the states-participants in the All-European Conference in Europe as it has been constituted and exists today.

The governments-participants in these consultations propose that these views be discussed within the framework of the preparatory work preceding the All-European Conference in the course of bilateral or multilateral consultations among interested states. They are of course willing to discuss any other suggestions aimed at the practical preparation and ensuring of the success of the All-European Conference.

The Ministers of Foreign Affairs express on behalf of their governments the conviction that in spite of certain still unresolved difficulties all issues pertaining to the preparation and holding of the All-European Conference whether they concern the agenda, range of participants or manner of convening the conference might be settled provided good will and sincere endeavour to achieve mutual understanding are shown.

The governments of the Bulgarian People's Republic, Hungarian People's Republic, German Democratic Republic, Polish People's Republic, Rumanian Socialist Republic, Union of Soviet Socialist Republics, and the Czechoslovak Socialist Republic call upon all European states to strive in the interest of the continent's peaceful future for a speedier convening of the All-European Conference which might in their opinion be held in Helsinki in the first half of 1970.

Moscow Communique of December 1969

A meeting of party and state leaders of the People's Republic of Bulgaria, the Hungarian People's Republic, the German Democratic Republic, the Polish People's Republic, the Socialist Republic of Rumania, the Union of Soviet Socialist Republics and the Czechoslovak Socialist Republic took place in Moscow on Dec. 3-4, 1969.

The participants in the meeting exchanged views on a wide range of problems connected with the consolidation of peace and international security. Special attention was given to questions of insuring security in Europe.

Satisfaction was expressed with the fact that extensive international support is being given to the proposals collectively drafted by socialist countries on preparing and holding an all-European conference of states.

Socialist countries will insistently press further for good neighborliness to replace tension on European soil, for peaceful coexistence to become a universal norm of mutual relations of European states with different social systems, for the striving of the peoples for security and progress to be embodied in concrete deeds, in the solution of topical problems of that part of the world.

The socialist countries taking part in the meeting come out for the expansion and development of relations between all states on the principles of equality, noninterference in internal affairs, respect of sovereignty, territorial integrity and inviolability of existing borders.

They are fully resolved to develop relations with other European states, wishing to cooperate on the basis of these principles.

Present Borders Stressed

They confirmed their opinion that the interests of peace and security demand that all states establish equal relations with the G.D.R. on the basis of international law and recognize the existing European borders, including the border along the Oder and Neisse, as final and unchangeable.

It was stated during the exchange of views on topical international questions that the election returns in the Federal Republic of Germany and the forming of the new Government are an expression of changes taking place among a part of the West German public, the growth among it of tendencies

Issued by the Party and state leaders of the seven active members of the Warsaw Pact (Albania excluded) following their summit meeting in Moscow on December 3-4, 1969; this translation appeared in the New York *Times* of December 5, 1969.

directed at a realistic policy of cooperation and mutual understanding among states.

The signing of the Federal Republic of Germany of the nuclear nonproliferation treaty should be noted as a positive feature.

At the same time the participants in the meeting expressed the unanimous view that the unceasing dangerous manifestations of revanchiem and the activisation of neo—Nazi forces in the F.R.G. must be kept constantly in mind and sober vigilance must be constantly maintained in respect of them.

If the new West German Government draws the lessons of history, rids itself of the ballast of the past and, acting in accordance with he spirit of the time, displays a realistic approach to problems creating tension in relations between European states, this will be welcomed both by socialist countries and by all peaceloving peoples.

Nuclear Treaty Backed

Believing it to be very important for the treaty on nuclear nonproliferation to serve in full measure the cause of strengthening peace, the People's Republic of Bulgaria, the Hungarian People's Republic, the German Democratic Republic, the Polish People's Republic, the Socialist Republic of Rumania, the Union of Soviet Socialist Republic and the Czechoslovak Socialist Republic come out for the accession to it of the biggest number of states, for the treaty's speediest ratification and entry into force.

The conviction was unanimously expressed that to insure a sound and stable peace it is necessary to advance along the road of ending the arms race and of general and complete disarmament, including nuclear disarmament.

Socialist countries, which have repeatedly made concrete proposals in this field, call on all states to display good will and readiness to commence in practice genuine disarmament.

The countries participating in the meeting again confirmed their desire to go on consulting each other on the most important problems of international life with the aim of carrying out concerted joint actions in the struggle for peace and the security of the peoples, including European security.

The Moscow meeting, which confirmed the identity of views of its participants, passed in an atmosphere of friendship, accord and comradely cooperation.

Notes

Notes to Chapter 2

1. For an interesting juxtaposition of views, see Ronald Steel's review of Dean Acheson's memoirs in the *New York Review of Books*, February 12, 1970.

2. See, for example, the article by Henry Owen in the Washington *Post* of January 26, 1970, and the Moscow dispatch from Anthony Astrachan in the *Post* of January 23, 1970.

3. For a comparison of survey data on this point, see Daniel Lerner and Morton Gordon, *Euratlantica: Changing Perspectives of the European Elites* (Cambridge, Mass.: M.I.T. Press, 1969), page 112, and Chapter 4 generally.

4. For a discussion of the varying meanings of this term in Soviet literature, see Raymond L. Garthoff, *Soviet Military Policy* (New York: Praeger, 1966), pages 78-91.

5. For a fuller historical comparison on the interesting similarities, see Robert E. Osgood and Robert W. Tucker, *Force, Order and Justice* (Baltimore: Johns Hopkins Press, 1967), page 201.

6. See Harlan Cleveland, *The Transatlantic Bargain* (forthcoming in 1970), Chapter 7. Ambassador Cleveland was United States Permanent Representative on the North Atlantic Council from 1965 to 1969 and kindly gave the authors an advance copy of the manuscript; references are therefore given to chapters only.

7. Timothy W. Stanley, *NATO in Transition* (New York: Praeger, for the Council on Foreign Relations, 1965) contains a brief overview of these developments in Chapter 2.

8. Statement of policy presented to the Bundestag, October 28, 1969. Extracts from the statement are translated and reprinted in *Survival*, volume xi, number 12, pages 370-373 (published by The Institute for Strategic Studies, London).

9. Foreign Secretary Michael Stewart made this suggestion during a Commons debate, in the course of rejecting the Prague proposal for a conference. British Information Services "Policy Statements," December 10, 1969.

10. See Leo Tujunen, "A Conference on European Security? Background to the Finnish Government's Proposal," *European Review* (London), volume xix, number 4 (Autumn 1969), pages 15-16.

Notes to Chapter 3

1. An analysis which is generally representative of this viewpoint is given in Richard J. Barnet and Marcus G. Raskin, *After 20 Years: The Decline of*

NATO and the Search for a New Policy in Europe (New York: Random House, 1965): for example, "the familiar landmarks that sustained the nightmare [of the Soviet threat to Europe] and the dream [of an Atlantic Community] are gone or profoundly altered" (page 4).

2. Adam Ulam calls the Treaty of Rapallo "the most important formal step in Soviet foreign policy between Brest-Litovsk and the Molotov-Ribbentrop agreement of 1939"; see his *Expansion and Coexistence: The History of Soviet Foreign Policy, 1917-1967* (New York: Praeger, 1968), page 149. Also see George F. Kennan, *Soviet Foreign Policy, 1917-1941* (New York: Van Nostrand, 1960), page 47; and Hajo Holborn, "Russia and the European Political System," *Russian Foreign Policy: Essays in Historical Perspective,* edited by Ivo J. Lederer (New Haven, Conn.: Yale University Press, 1962), pages 411-412.

3. This pithy statement is made by Wilfrid Knapp in an essay entitled "The Partition of Europe" in Evan Luard, ed., *The Cold War: A Re-appraisal* (New York: Praeger, 1964), page 46.

4. For the official documents which established the Allied Control Council and the Reparations Commission, see "Agreement on Control Machinery in Germany," dated November 14, 1944 (and amendments) and "Protocol on the Talks Between the Heads of the Three Governments at the Crimean Conference on the Question of the German Reparation in Kind," both published as part of the proceedings of the Yalta Conference, held in February 1945. The texts of both agreements are given in *Documents on Germany, 1944-1961* (U.S., Congress, Senate, Committee on Foreign Relations, Committee Print, 87th Congress, 1st Session, December 1961).

5. Regarding Molotov's filibustering tactics, Secretary of State Byrnes observed,

> I have been forced to the conclusion that following Stalin's promise on December 24, 1945, to support the treaty, the Soviet High Command or Politburo concluded they did not want the United States involved in the maintenance of European security for the next twenty-five to forty years. The pressure of American power would restrict the freedom of action which the Soviet Union, as the predominant military power in Europe, might otherwise enjoy.

See James F. Byrnes, *Speaking Frankly* (New York: Harper, 1947), page 176.

6. The Soviet outline of a peace treaty with Germany, in the form of the "Note from the Soviet Government to the Three Western Powers, 10 March 1952," is published as Appendix One to *Disengagement* by Eugene Hinterhoff (London: Stevens, 1959). Hinterhoff's comprehensive study of the European security problem from 1945 to 1958 is particularly useful as a standard reference source, since nine of the major East-West proposals are printed as appendixes, supplemented by a lengthy table of Western and Eastern plans for security arrangements in Europe.

7. This specific appellation is that of Donald Watt in his essay on Germany in Luard, page 117.

8. See Hinterhoff, page 181, for this statement, which Secretary Dulles made on November 8, 1955.

9. Ibid., pages 177-236, 417-424, and 436-440. Hinterhoff provides an extensively detailed review of many of these plans. Other references are Bernard G. Bechoeffer, *Postwar Negotiations for Arms Control* (Washington: Brookings, 1961); and Lincoln Bloomfield et al., *Khrushchev and the Arms Race: Soviet Interests in Arms Control and Disarmament, 1954-1966* (Cambridge, Mass.: M.I.T. Press, 1966).

10. For example, see Barnet and Raskin, which calls for replacement of "the system of rival alliances" by a "new security system" based on "a European security treaty which would obligate the United States, the Soviet Union, and the European powers to respond to any threat to European security from any direction" (page 95). The authors do not note that mere adherence to the precepts of the United Nations Charter would accomplish the same objective; nor do they explain why the substantially similar proposal made many times over the past two decades failed to end the "obsolete pattern of alliances and arms races" and "end the war system for conducting international relations."

For a more balanced study of the issues in the European security problem, see the excellent critical evaluation of a number of models of European security systems by Pierre Hassner, *Change and Security in Europe, Part I: The Background* and *Part II: In Search of a System* (London: Institute for Strategic Studies, Adelphi Paper Number 45, February 1968, and Adelphi Paper Number 49, July 1968).

11. See Arnold Horelick and Myron Rush, *Strategic Power and Soviet Foreign Policy* (Chicago: University of Chicago Press, 1966).

12. This observation is made by Charles R. Planck in *The Changing Status of German Reunification in Western Diplomacy, 1955-1966,* Washington Center of Foreign Policy Research, Studies in International Affairs, No. 4 (Baltimore: Johns Hopkins Press, 1967), pages 43-44.

13. The text of President de Gaulle's press conference of February 4, 1965, may be found in *Speeches and Press Conferences* (New York: Ambassade de France, Service de Presse et d'Information, Number 216).

14. The "Peace Note of the Federal Government of 25 March 1966 to All States" appears on page 6 of *The Policy of Renunciation of Force, Documents on German and Soviet Declarations on the Renunciation of Force, 1949 to July 1968* (Bonn: Press and Information Office of the Federal Government, July 1968). A special issue of *Survey* (London), number 61 (October 1966), entitled "Germany: Today and Tomorrow," contains a

number of excellent articles on the development of the Grand Coalition's foreign policy. See the contributions by Pierre Hassner, Ekkehardt Krippendorff, Peter Bender, Hans Speier, and William Griffith.

15. This analysis of Soviet proposals from 1966 through 1969 relies extensively on an article by Marshall D. Shulman, "A European Security Conference," *Europa Archiv, Folge* 19 (1969), reprinted in *Survival,* volume xi, number 12 (December 1969), pages 373-382.

16. Extracts from the Brandt Government's policy statement appear in *The German Tribune, A Weekly Review of the German Press* (Hamburg), number 396 (November 11, 1969), page 3.

17. For Senator Mansfield's comments to the Senate and the text of Senate Resolution 292, see the *Congressional Record* of December 1, 1969, pages S15162-S15168.

18. Secretary Rogers' speech was issued by the State Department as Release Number 369 (Revised), dated December 6, 1969.

19. The report of Zamyatin's news conference was printed in the New York *Times* of January 14, 1970, pages 1 and 12.

20. Dispatches from Belgrade and Moscow indicated this disaffection by leaders of Communist parties in East and West Europe; see the Washington *Post* of January 23 and January 26, 1970.

Notes to Chapter 4

1. See Winston S. Churchill, *The Second World War* (Boston: Houghton Mifflin, 1953), Volume 5, *Closing the Ring,* page 400. As Churchill records the discussion,

> Stalin now asked: "Are there any other questions?" The President replied, "There is the question of Germany." Stalin said that he would like to see Germany split up. The President agreed, but Stalin suggested that I should object. I said I did not.

Roosevelt's idea for dismembering Germany into five separate states was then discussed on the basis of general agreement in principle, but no decisions were taken.

2. Ibid., Volume 6, *Triumph and Tragedy,* page 497.

3. The Preface to *Documents on Germany Under Occupation 1945-1954,* edited by Beate Ruhm von Oppen (London: Oxford University Press, published for the Royal Institute of International Affairs, 1955), page v, expresses, with typically British understatement, the frustrations of the translator: "The linguistic revolution which has taken place in the Russian Zone of Germany . . . is less a Russian influence than an ideological one . . . old words have assumed a new meaning."

4. Secretary Marshall's report on the Fifth Session of Foreign Ministers, held on December 19, 1947, can be found in *Documents on Germany, 1944-1961*, page 82.

5. Austria eventually received a peace treaty, and her sovereignty was restored and occupation forces withdrawn in 1955.

6. *Documents on Germany, 1944-1961*, page 98.

7. *Documents on Germany Under Occupation, 1945-1954*, page 120.

8. Good accounts of these developments can be found in Gerald Freund, *Germany Between Two Worlds* (New York: Harcourt, 1961); and in Manuel Gottlieb, *The German Peace Settlement and the Berlin Crisis* (New York: Paine-Whitman, 1960).

9. The full texts of the key Paris agreements can be found as Appendixes 9 and 10 in *NATO Facts and Figures*.

10. For a good account of the 1955-1966 period, see Planck.

11. Chancellor Brandt's views as Foreign Minister are contained in his book *A Peace Policy for Europe* (New York: Holt, 1968). His views as Chancellor are summarized in his policy statement to the Bundestag of October 28, 1969 (excerpted in *Survival*, volume xi, number 12, December 1969, pages 370-373; and in assorted press reports); see also his speech to the Bundestag on January 14, 1970, reported in the New York *Times* of January 15, 1970.

12. Brzezinski's concept is spelled out in his *Alternative to Partition* (New York: McGraw-Hill, 1965) and, more recently, in an article in the Washington *Post* of January 18, 1970, page B-5.

13. The Soviets have continued to maintain that Berlin is a quadripartite responsibility in the context of European security; see the Zamyatin press conference statement.

14. The complete record of international agreements giving the West unrestricted military access to Berlin is contained in *Documents on Germany, 1944-1961*, especially pages 23-54, 623, 625, and 756.

15. See the New York *Times* of January 26, 1970, page 7.

16. The Soviets and East Germans began their harassment of West German political activities in West Berlin, for example, meetings of the Bundestag or its committees, only in the 1960's—having never objected to numerous meetings until 1959—and have regularly allowed the East German Volks-kammer to meet in East Berlin. See *Documents on Germany, 1944-1961*, page 651.

17. For example, see the speech by Dr. Karl Pfleiderer, an FDP member of the Bundestag, on June 6, 1952, reported in Hinterhoff, pages 156-158.

18. See the Washington *Post* of February 11, 1970, page A-4; and the New York *Times* dispatches by David Binder of February 11 and February 12, 1970.

19. See the article by Colonel General K. Skorobvogatkin, "The U.S.S.R. Does Not Have a Military Industrial Complex," *Red Star*, December 28, 1969. The contrary evidence and the case that the Russian "complex" has "absolute priority" over the civilian sectors of the economy are compiled in Richard Armstrong, "Military-Industrial Complex-Russian Style," *Fortune*, volume 80, number 2 (August 1, 1969), page 85.

20. Malcolm Mackintosh reports:

> The Soviet Union has lately renewed her original twenty-year bilateral mutual aid treaties with the East European countries, in many cases ahead of time. There is also a series of interlocking treaties between the East European countries themselves. . . . While these bilateral treaties are described in the Soviet press as "an organic part of the agreements uniting the socialist states of Europe, the Warsaw Pact and the Council for Mutual Economic Aid", there can be no doubt that they also form a "reserve" series of alliances which could keep the Warsaw Pact in being if it should ever become necessary for the Soviet Union to agree to its formal disbandment.

See *The Evolution of the Warsaw Pact* (London: Institute for Strategic Studies, Adelphi Paper Number 58, June 1969), page 18 and Appendix C, page 25. Appendix C is entitled "East European Bilateral Treaty System (Treaties of Friendship, Co-operation and Mutual Assistance) [of the seven active members of the Warsaw Pact, Albania excluded]."

21. Cleveland, "NATO After the Invasion," *Foreign Affairs*, volume 47, number 2 (January 1969), page 254.

22. These figures are taken from *The Military Balance, 1969-1970* (London: Institute for Strategic Studies, 1969); and from the "Defense Posture" statement in "Fiscal Year 1971 Defense Program and Budget," message delivered by Secretary of Defense Melvin R. Laird to a joint session of the Senate committees on Armed Services and Appropriations on February 20, 1970 (Washington: Government Printing Office, 1970), Appendix C.

23. The pessimists are represented by Lord Wigg (former Paymaster General) in the London *Times* of February 20, 1969; and by General Graf Kielmansegg and, to a lesser extent, Denis Healey in their articles in *Orbis*, volume xiii, number 1 (Spring 1969). The optimists' view is well represented by Alain B. Enthoven's article in *Foreign Affairs*, volume 48, number 1, (October 1969), pages 80-97, and his earlier, more detailed treatment in *Interplay*, volume 2, number 10 (May 1969), pages 11-14.

24. Under Secretary Richardson's address to the Chicago Council on Foreign Relations took place on Tuesday, January 20, 1970; see the New York *Times* of January 21, 1970.

25. The Washington *Post* of January 24, 1970, page A-10.

26. There seem to be various definitions of "substantial." The Washington *Post* of February 9, 1970, quotes Senator Percy as saying that Senator Mansfield has in mind one hundred thousand men, presumably two full division slices and their support; see also the New York *Times* of February 4, 1970, and the *Congressional Record* of December 1, 1969, page S15162.

27. See Secretary Laird's statement, page 26.

28. Estimates of all direct, NATO-related costs to the United States— excluding American strategic nuclear forces which would be maintained in any case—range from twelve to fourteen billion dollars annually. (The budgetary cost of American forces actually in Europe, however, is only about two and a half billion to two billion eight hundred million dollars per year.) The other NATO members' total defense spending in 1969 is estimated at twenty-three billion three hundred million dollars, including France. However, some of this, perhaps as much as three billion dollars, was not expended specifically for "NATO" purposes—just as in the case of the United States, where much of the defense budget is not NATO related. Thus, the current American share of the total NATO defense burden can range from a low fraction of 12/35ths, or thirty-three percent (where no reduction is made for the Europeans' non-NATO expenditures) to a high fraction of 14/29ths, or forty-eight percent (where France's five billion six hundred million dollars is excluded.) A twelve billion dollar figure (for all American "NATO-oriented" forces) is used by Enthoven; see also the syndicated column by Robert Allen and John Goldsmith of January 28, 1970. The European figures are taken from *The Military Balance, 1969-1970.*

In terms of NATO's forces, excluding France, the United States provides approximately one tenth of ground forces, one fifth of air forces, and up to one third of the Navy (though much of the latter contribution is "on call," rather than assigned). This does not seem a disproportionate share for the world's most powerful nation, although of course it does not take account of the strategic nuclear umbrella which the United States also furnishes its Western European allies.

29. See Secretary Laird's statement, page 54.

30. This information about the British White Paper on defense is reported in the Washington *Star* of February 19, 1970.

31. For a full account, including the financial estimates (based on State and Defense Department testimony to Congressional committees), see Eric Stein and Dominique Carreau, "Law and Peaceful Change in a Subsystem:

'Withdrawal' of France from the North Atlantic Treaty Organization,"
American Journal of International Law, volume 62, number 3 (July 1968),
pages 626 and 636.

32. See the Washington *Post* of January 24, 1970, page A-15.

33. Alstair Buchan and Philip Windsor, *Arms and Stability in Europe*
(London: Chatto and Windus, for the Institute for Strategic Studies, 1963),
was one of the earlier comprehensive works. Hassner explored various models;
Karl Birnbaum of Sweden reviewed "Ways Towards European Security,"
Europa Archiv, Folge 7 (1968), reprinted in *Survival,* volume x, number 6
(June 1968), pages 193-200, and suggested a four-stage all-European security
system. The Centre d'Etudes de Politique Etrangere and the Institute for
Strategic Studies have both examined alternative models for European
security, some of which involved mutual force reductions.

34. One former SACEUR believes that the high quality of American forces
makes them the worst element with which to begin reduction on the Western
side, because there would be a disproportionate cut in NATO combat
readiness. He also opposes any unilateral "setting of an example"; if the
Western reduction were not reciprocated by the Warsaw Pact, the NATO
posture would be badly weakened. Another observer stresses the importance
of the international aspects within NATO—as well as in East-West terms—in
order to maintain the Alliance solidarity on which the entire scheme depends;
see the comments of General Lyman L. Lemnitzer and Professor Robert S.
Jordan, respectively, in Stanley, *A European Security Conference?—
Problems, Prospects, and Pitfalls* (Washington: Atlantic Council, 1970),
Appendix Three.

35. Under Secretary Richardson's view of the redeployment option (see Note
24 to this chapter) indicates that the Nixon Administration regards it less
favorably than did its predecessor. Richardson suggests that return of
American forces to Europe in a time of crisis reduces their effectiveness and
exposes them to hazards. The background of this redeployment is given in
Cleveland, *The Transatlantic Bargain.*

36. Comments by Admiral Robert L. Dennison on this point are in Stanley, *A
European Security Conference?,* Appendix Three.

37. For an explanation of these terms, which we prefer to the label "flexible
response," see Stanley, "A Strategic Doctrine for NATO in the 1970's,"
Orbis, volume xiii, number 1 (Spring 1969), pages 87-100.

38. Ibid. For comprehensive treatments, see Walter Schutze, *European
Defense Co-operation in NATO* (Paris: The Atlantic Institute, 1969); and
Geoffrey Ashcroft, *Military Logistic Systems in NATO: The Goal of
Integration,* (London: The Institute for Strategic Studies, Adelphi Paper
Number 62, November 1969).

39. According to a Washington *Post* story of February 9, 1970, Soviet Ambassador Dobrynin expressed interest in mutual force reductions during a call on Under Secretary of State Richardson.

40. SALT has been covered widely in the American press; good summaries can be found in the New York *Times* of November 17, 1969, and *Newsweek*, November 24, 1969, page 47. The Nixon Administration's view is contained both in Secretary Laird's "posture" statement and in the President's message, "A United States Foreign Policy for the 1970's: A New Strategy for Peace," dated February 18, 1970. This message was reprinted in the New York *Times* of February 19, 1970, and as "Message from the President of the United States Transmitting a Report on Foreign Relations" (U.S., Congress, House, Committee on Foreign Affairs, House Document Number 91-258, 91st Congress, 2d Session, February 18, 1970). Subsequent page references are to this House Document.

41. See the President's message, page 146.

42. Shulman, page 378.

43. See the story by William Beecher in the New York *Times* of February 11, 1970, page 10.

44. This has been a particular interest of the United Kingdoms; see, for example, the article by Lord Chalfont in the *European Review*, volume xviii, number 4 (Autumn 1968).

45. The Federal Government's Press and Information Office has published two collections of documents on the subject. The quotation is found on page 16 of *The Policy of Renunciation of Force, Documents on German and Soviet Declarations on the Renunciation of Force, 1949 to July 1968*, which was issued after the Soviets published some of their demarches. The second collection, *For Peace and Relaxation of Tensions: Documents on German Efforts for Peace and Relaxation of Tensions, 1949 up to August 1968*, partially overlaps the first source but carries the exchanges through August 1968.

46. The *Pravda* article of September 26, 1968, by Sergei Kovalyov is reprinted in *Survival*, volume x, number 11 (November 1968), which is devoted to the Soviet invasion of Czechoslovakia.

47. See Milan Bartos, "The Aggression," *Review of International Affairs* (Yugoslavia), September 5, 1968.

48. This point is discussed in *The German Tribune, A Weekly Review of the German Press*, number 405 (January 13, 1970).

49. The Soviet insistence that the Munich agreement was "invalid from the very beginning—together with all the consequences flowing from it,"—(as well

as the tie to mutual force renunciations) is spelled out in the Soviet Memorandum to the Federal Republic of November 21, 1967, and its enclosures. These are reprinted in *The Policy of Renunciation of Force*, pages 9-15.

50. Brzezinski, *Alternative to Partition*, page 49.

51. Czechoslovakia had been an original member before the Communist take over in 1948; she has since been inactive. See *The Battle Act Report, 1968*, Twenty-First Report to Congress under the Mutual Defense Assistance Control Act of 1951 (Department of State Publication 8426, January 1969), pages 19-20. This is the latest Battle Act Report available at this writing. The first report under the Nixon Administration is expected to be published in the spring of 1970.

52. See Clyde H. Farnsworth's dispatch in the New York *Times* of February 6, 1970.

53. See *The Battle Act Report, 1968*.

54. For example, one of the largest East-West trade agreements was the five hundred million dollar arrangement whereby Fiat will build an automobile factory in Russia in exchange for shipments of natural gas. More recently, Bonn has financed a twenty-year, seven hundred million dollar arrangement whereby German steel pipe (on NATO's strategic embargo list until a few years ago) will be exchanged for some three billion cubic meters of natural gas annually, delivered via a pipeline through Czechoslovakia. See the Washington *Post* of February 2, 1970, page A-1. To be competitive with North Sea gas, the Russians are apparently willing to accept very low wellhead prices, in view of the distances involved from the Ukraine and Siberia.

55. The Senate Foreign Relations Committee has held numerous hearings on East-West trade; for example, see the Committee Print *East-West Trade, A Compilation of Views of Businessmen, Bankers, and Academic Experts* (88th Congress, 2d Session, 1964) and *East-West Trade, Hearings* (89th Congress, 1st Session, 1965).

56. See *The Battle Act Report, 1968*.

57. Garst's observations are contained in a letter to Senator Fulbright, printed in *East-West Trade, A Compilation of Views*, pages 5-8.

58. Figures on travel can be found in the *United Nations Statistical Yearbook*, usually with a lag of a year or two; those used here are generalizations from Table 163 of the 1968 edition.

59. See the New York *Times* of February 11, 1970, page 9.

Notes to Chapter 5

1. See Michel Tatu, "What the Russians Hope to Gain from Next Year's Negotiations," *Le Monde,* (Weekly Selection, English) December 10, 1969).

2. Some observers of the East German propaganda drive—for Western diplomatic recognition and for a conference—through the German labor unions feel that the danger is acute. See "Zum Tage," *Die Welt,* January 5, 1970; and "Die Rolle des DGB im kommunistischen Planspiel," *Die Welt* January 6, 1970.

3. The *Fortune* survey suggests a substantial influence, drawing on data from RAND, SRI, and the U.S. Government. See also Alexander Dallin, "Soviet Foreign Policy and Domestic Politics: A Framework for Analysis," Columbia University *Journal of International Affairs,* volume 23, November 2, 1969.

4. Cleveland, *The Transatlantic Bargain,* Chapter 8.

5. According to the Moscow story by Anthony Astrachan in the Washington *Post* of January 23, 1970, "at least six Communist parties quarrelled with the Soviet Union" at the January 15-16, 1970, meeting of party delegates to discuss a European security conference.

6. Cleveland, *The Transatlantic Bargain,* Chapter 8.

7. See the New York *Times* of the Zamyatin press conference.

8. Shulman, pages 380 and 381.

9. For a general review of international negotiations and tactics, see Fred C. Ikle, *How Nations Negotiate* (New York: Praeger, 1964).

10. See Tujunen, pages 15 and 16.

11. *Toward the Reconciliation of Europe, New Approaches for the U.S., the UN and NATO,* A Report of a National Policy Panel established by the United Nations Association of the United States (New York: The United Nations Association, January 1969).

Notes to Chapter 6

1. House of Commons Foreign Affairs Debate, December 9, 1969.

2. Andrei Amalrick, *Will the Soviet Union Survive until 1984?* (New York: Harper, 1970).

3. The President's message of February 18, 1970, page 134.

4. For an incisive discussion of the relationship of SALT to NATO, see Robert L. Pfaltzgraff, Jr., "Superpower-Ally Relationships: The United

States-*NATO*-Europe," a paper presented to the Fourth International Arms Control Symposium held in Philadelphia October 17-19, 1969.

5. The President's message of February 18, 1970.

6. In this speech to the North Atlantic Assembly at Brussels on October 18, 1969, Secretary General Brosio also sounded cautionary notes about the effects of the Pact's proposals for a security conference and about Soviet motivations; but he noted that NATO's official policy, as embodied in the Harmel report, *is* one of Western initiatives.

7. For interesting comment on de-emphasizing Soviet motivations and concentrating on the West's opportunities, see the comment by Thomas W. Wilson, Jr., in Stanley, *A European Security Conference?*, Appendix Three.

About the Authors

Timothy W. Stanley is visiting Professor of International Relations at The Johns Hopkins University School of Advanced International Studies (SAIS) and Research Associate of the Washington Center of Foreign Policy Research. He returned last summer from Europe, after serving for over four years as Assistant to the Secretary of Defense for NATO Force Planning and Defense Advisor at the United States Mission, with the personal rank of Minister. He received the Defense Department's Distinguished Civilian Service Medal for his work at NATO. He was a member of the White House staff from 1957 to 1959 and served in various capacities on the staffs of the last six Secretaries of Defense. A graduate of Yale and a veteran of two tours of duty in the Army, Professor Stanley holds both an LL.B. and a Ph.D. from Harvard; he is the author of *American Defense and National Security, NATO in Transition,* and numerous articles on foreign and defense policy. He is a member of the Connecticut Bar, the Council on Foreign Relations, the Institute for Strategic Studies, the American Academy of Political and Social Science, and the American Political Science Association, and has taught at Harvard, George Washington, and Johns Hopkins universities.

Darnell M. Whitt is conducting research at the Center while completing his doctoral dissertation at Johns Hopkins. A graduate of Harvard, he served in Europe and the Far East for nearly five years as an officer in the regular Navy and is a former member of the Policy Planning Staff of the Assistant Secretary of Defense (International Security Affairs) and of the United States Mission to NATO in Paris and Brussels. He is a member of the Institute for Strategic Studies and the American Political Science Association. He has studied abroad, holds a master's degree from SAIS, and has taught courses in national security affairs and contemporary European diplomacy.